.

BORN
IN AN
UNKNOWN
HOUR

www.royalcollins.com

BORN IN AN UNKNOWN HOUR

*A Selection of
Fan Xiaoqing's
Short Stories*

FAN XIAOQING

Books Beyond Boundaries

ROYAL COLLINS

Born in an Unknown Hour: A Selection of Fan Xiaoqing's Short Stories

FAN XIAOQING

First published in 2021 by Royal Collins Publishing Group Inc.
Groupe Publication Royal Collins Inc.
BKM Royalcollins Publishers Private Limited

Headquarters: 550-555 boul. René-Lévesque O Montréal (Québec) H2Z1B1 Canada
India office: 805 Hemkunt House, 8th Floor, Rajendra Place, New Delhi 110008

Original Edition © Nanjing Normal University Press was included in the series
"A Bilingual Library Contemporary Chinese Master Writers", edited by Yang
Haocheng and Li Zhongtao.

This English edition is authorized by Nanjing Normal University Press.

ISBN: 978-1-4878-0809-9

To find out more about our publications, please visit www.royalcollins.com

PREFACE

D o college students read today? Certainly they do, but what do they read? They surf the net, they read text messages, and they get bogged down in an ocean of information from blogs or WeChat. They seem to read extensively, but much they read and enjoy reading is nothing but sheer guff and hogwash. They know something about everything, but nothing they know seems to be of any substantial depth or breadth. With their mobile phones constantly in their hands at every moment, they are phubbing all those around them. The tiny machine makes its way to the classroom, where it replaces the textbook as the most eye-catching and attention-drawing plaything to the hopeless stare of the teachers. "The textbook is full of corrupt stuff anyway," I recall with astonishment my late advisor Jessie Chambers saying years ago, when she was asked to give her opinion on China's college education.

So it is fragmented reading from the new media that college students seem to be enjoying today, and serious literature is woefully slighted or neglected, forgotten in the dust-covered shelves of the libraries, becoming spiritual food for a minority of bookish souls. When it comes to English learning, the situation is no more encouraging. Chinese students do not read serious literature anymore. What they have learned is gibberish full of "kind of," or internet jive and cants, some pop songs, and an exaggerated show of shrugs. They count themselves fluent in English, not knowing that a real command of the foreign tongue is built on an extensive reading of good literature of all kinds.

Talking of extracurricular reading, I remember what I saw when my wife and I visited her cousin eleven years ago in New York. She had a son and a daughter. The boy, Franklin, was an undergraduate of the University of Pennsylvania, and the girl, Shelly, having just finished her elementary school, was awaiting with great excitement her commencement, which we all attended the next day. Out of curiosity, I flipped through Shelly's reading materials. I saw Shakespeare, Milton, Mark Twain, Hemingway, and other renowned writers lying helter-skelter on her reading table. There was also a copy of *Harry Potter,* of course. I asked Shelly, "You're reading these?" "Yes, for fun!" she snapped. An elementary school pupil reading Shakespeare, Milton, Mark Twain, and Hemingway outside the classroom! And for fun! What are our college students reading? This question has weighed upon me like a leaden slab over the years.

Maybe American students aren't a good comparison? Let's look instead, then, at the contents of Freshman Readings in English for undergraduate students at the National Southwestern Associated University in war-torn China. Mind you, this was for all the freshmen, not just those majoring in English. Compiled by Prof Chen Futian, a Hawaii-born Harvard ME, the Readings had a total of 43 essays, almost all written by master hands and which smack of a strong spirit of liberal education. The Readings were vastly different from the so-called "Practical English," "Business English," "Legal English," "Secretarial English," and other such courses prevalent in college classrooms today. They included "Barren Spring" by Pearl S. Buck, "Beast of Burden" and "Song of the River" by W. Somerset Maugham, "Birth of a Sister" by Tan Shih-hua, "A Dissertation upon Roast Pig" by Charles Lamb, "An Optimistic Look at China" by Hu Shih, "The End of Life" by Lin Yutang, "A Sacred Mountain" by G. Lowes Dickinson, "Fragments from a Flower Diary" by Nora Waln, "A Word to Youth" by Andre Maurois, "A Pair of Woodpeckers" by an unknown author, "The Battle of the Red and the Black Ants" by Henry David Thoreau, "Liberty" by Woodrow Wilson, "What Is Science?" by Ira Remsen, "The Durable Satisfactions of Life" by Charles W. Eliot, "The Imaginary Invalid" by Jerome K. Jerome, "The Tell-Tale Heart" by Edgar Allan Poe, "The Widow and Her Son" by Washington Irving, "The Champion Snorer" by an unknown author, "A Liberal Education" by Thomas Henry Huxley, "The Function of Education in Democratic Society" by Charles W. Eliot, "What Shall We Educate for?" by Bertrand Russell, "The Strength of Democracy" by Walter Lippmann, "Technological Civilization" by Charles A. Beard, "The Social Value of the College-Bred" by William James, "Liberty and Discipline" by Abbot Lawrence Lowell, "The Liberation of a People's Vital Energies" by Woodrow Wilson, "Habit" by William James, "Why a Classic is a Classic" by Arnold Bennett, "Evolution" by John Galsworthy, "Fighting in Gallipoli" by John Masefield, "The Half Mile" by T. O. Beachcroft, "The Long Shadow" by John Hampson, "The Field Where the Satyrs Danced" by Lord Dunsany, "Every Man's Natural Desire to Be Somebody Else" by Samuel McChord Crothers, "The Philosopher" by W. Somerset Maugham, "Bismarck" by Emil Ludwig, "The Riddle of Hitler" by Stephen H. Roberts, "British Foreign Policy" by John Gunther, "The American Love of Freedom" by Edmund Burke, "What is a University?" by John Henry Newman, "Theory of the Liberal College" by Alexander Meiklejohn, and "Self-Cultivation in English" by George Herbert Palmer. And these are just freshman readings. Just imagine what the students would be like after four years of intensive reading of arts and letters like these.

You would say that most of these are foreign literature, and our students are Chinese, and as Chinese they must be well versed in their mother tongue or well read in Chinese literature. Not at all! I find to my dismay that today's Chinese college students haven't read anything of Chinese literary classics. I used to teach a course entitled Translation of Literary Classics. Among all the English and Chinese materials I'd prepared, nothing seemed to have been on the students' reading list except perhaps Lu Xun's "Kong Yiji," which was in their middle school textbook. They're well acquainted with, say, the names of the "Four Literary Masterpieces," but not many of them have bothered to read any of them. Taoist and Confucian classics such as *Daodejing* (Classics of the Way and Virtue), *Zhuangzi*, *The Analects*, *Mencius*, *The Great Learning*, and *The Doctrine of the Golden Mean* were all must reads of any school kids in olden days, but today, they are even more out of the question. Today's students claim that their teachings are too far detached from real life and their mode of linguistic expression is miserably esoteric to modern readers.

This situation is discouraging enough, but it is against this gloomy background that A Bilingual Library of Contemporary Chinese Master Writers has been launched by Nanjing Normal University Press, in hopes of bringing back some of the lost lambs to the conventional mode of paper book reading. However, our target readers are not limited to college students, and anyone who might be interested in Chinese-English translation, comparative literature, and comparative studies between Chinese and Western cultures may find their own rewards in reading from the Library, for which there are two points to say at the least. First, the present Library was born amidst the favorable climate of Chinese culture Going Global which, as a top-down, nationwide, and now largely canonized slogan, was a significant factor in its publication. It is natural that when a country has earned a stronghold in the world economy, as China has now done so robustly, it will desire to go all out in other respects, including culture. Historically, it has been true of such institutions as the Alliance Française, the British Council, and the Goethe-Institut, all important channels for their respective countries' cultural flow and interaction. It is probably a matter of national self-confidence and pride, but there is nothing wrong with that. The question that remains is how a country's culture should go global. Two forces are at work: various bureaucrats, and professionals such as researchers, writers, translators, editors, and publishers. The two forces have the same aim, but sadly, each espouses different strategies and approaches for introducing their cultural achievements to the outside world. Largely ignorant of the foreign languages and their cultures, bureaucrats want very much to sell what they deem to be precious material to a potential buyer, not knowing that cultural exchange is, to a great extent, like trade and is built on the basis of equal give-and-take and willingness on the side of the buyer, while any one-sided forced selling is doomed to fail. Though much more informed, the professionals are reliant on the bureaucrats for political direction and financial support, and are thus left in a dilemma. They want to proceed with what they regard as the right path, but are frequently met with undesirable obstacles, including unwelcomed directions or interferences from the bureaucrats. The case of *Chinese Literature,* an officially sponsored magazine that has struggled for a full fifty years, is instructive. Though *CL* has had as its chief editor the prolific, charismatic translator Yang Xianyi for the second half of its fifty-year life, Yang alone certainly would not have had sufficient strength to stay clear of the political influences of his day. *CL* bears the clear hallmark of its time, which explains its low readership overseas over the years.

Fortunately, the present *Library* is able to adhere to its set standard, and what is collected here are either representative works or highly recognized pieces of some of the most famous writers from contemporary China. After the lapse of dozens of years of ideological struggles, we are able to return at last to the ontological study of literary creation, and all the works translated here speak of the commonality of human nature and human life – humankind's happiness, anger, sorrow, and joy – despite their vastly different approaches and perspectives toward literature. With their succinct style, exquisite structure, and typical characters and events, these stories constitute an extremely important, integral part of the treasure house of contemporary Chinese literature. For a better, more three-dimensional presentation of the authors and their works, we have also included a critique and an interview for each author, with only a few exceptions.

In addition, it is common knowledge among translators that they do better when translating into their mother tongue. It's an undeniable fact that translators whose mother tongue is English will be much more at home when it comes to Chinese-English translation. Professor Yang Haocheng used to call Sidney Shapiro about his translation of *Outlaws of the Marsh*. Mr Shapiro once said to him on the phone, "Translating things like *Outlaws of the Marsh* is much easier for me than translating English materials into Chinese. After all, Chinese is not my mother tongue, though I became a Chinese citizen all the way back in 1963."

The present *Library* boasts a terrific pool of professional translators whose mother tongue is English, and all of them are bilingual or multilingual. They are the same translators who are working for *Chinese Arts & Letters*. This makes all the difference. In fact, both *Chinese Literature* and almost all other journals and magazines run by Chinese publishers have the same problem. Many of their translators are non-native speakers or writers of the target language, and their English was learned as a second language. They cannot be compared with professional translators whose mother tongue is English and, better still, whose command of the Chinese language is superb. Many of them are internationally recognized sinologists or old China hands to boot. Denis Mair, Nicky Harman, Natascha Bruce, Luisetta Mudie, Shelly Bryant, Josh Stenberg, Helen Wang, Jeremy Tiang, Eric Abrahamsen, Michael Day, Simon Patton, and Florence Woo are among our most conscientious and treasured translators. What comes out of their hands may seem at first glance to be nothing special, yet their work is so idiomatic and reads so comfortably that we cannot help but admire.

The target audience of the present *Library*, then, should first of all be readers interested in translation, especially undergraduates and graduate students studying translation. When Professor Yang Haocheng was reading the manuscripts prepared by these translators, he often could not keep himself from copying their wonderful translations with careful analysis, such as the rendering of, "她有着凹凸有致的身材" (meaning "she has a figure of voluptuous curves"). There is a special word, albeit highly colloquial, to describe that kind of girl, "zaftig." So we constantly hear people say, "She is a sort of zaftig, coquettish girl." Similarly, "包二奶" is a very common term today, and our translator renders it, "to keep a bit on the side." Accordingly, "当小三" is "to be somebody's bit on the side," "bit" meaning a loose woman, and "on the side," in secret or on the sly, but with a bit of humor. Likewise, "吃货," a term enjoyed by many young people today, has also its English equivalent, "greedy guts." (Mind you, it's *guts* and not *gut*. For instance: *He is a greedy guts.*) This is aside from other possible renderings, such as foodie, glutton, gourmand, gastronaut, or food aficionado, as listed by the most advanced Chinese-English Dictionary chief-edited by the late Professor Lu Gusun. And "恶搞" actually has a Japanese term "to kuso," which has already entered the English language, making "to parody," "to lampoon," and "to snark" seem somewhat outdated. "Phubber," the reverse formation of "phubbing," which is said to be a new coinage by some Australian linguists, lexicographers, and authors from "phone" and "snub," a neologism to describe the habit of snubbing people around you in favor of a mobile phone, is an exact equivalent of the popular Chinese term "低头族." It only has a history of five years, and though already included in the Australian National Dictionary, most other dictionaries or thesauruses have not yet included it. And such simple oral sayings as "过了这村儿没这店儿" and "金窝银窝, 不如自家狗窝" are masterfully translated into the pithy phrase, "It's now or never," and the most faithful to date, "Gold dish, silver dish, they cannot compare to your own dog's dish," respectively, both genius outgrowths from the prosaic "last chance," and the equally memorable – though losing the image – clause, "East or west, home is best." This alone is a good reason why the *Library* is a good read for all who are interested in translation. In fact, editing these works has turned out to be a great opportunity for us editors to learn about the two languages, and it has generally uplifted us. Many universities have chosen the *Library* as the textbook for their translation courses and have included it in the list of reference books for the entrance examination for their Masters in Translation and Interpretation programs.

The target audience of *A Bilingual Library of Contemporary Chinese Master Writers* also includes scholars of comparative literature and comparative study of the cultures of East and West. With systematic planning, organization, and support, the quantity and quality of translations of Chinese literature have greatly improved. However, their influence overseas is still limited, and Chinese literature in translation is still not an "active presence" in World Literature. We believe that the key to addressing this problem is to emphasize not only international translation of Chinese literature, but also international literary criticism. At the Symposium on Chinese Literature Going Global since Mo Yan Won the Nobel Prize, Professor Song Binghui pointed out that "for Chinese literature to really go global, it must, to a large extent, depend on literary scholars' interpretation of the literary works, and having effective multiple interpretations of the literary works is an important factor in realizing the internationalization of local literature." When contemporary Chinese literature has been introduced to the world, this dimension has not received due attention, so we are trying to achieve a breakthrough in this area. After Professor Yang Haocheng passed away, we invited Professor Sheng Ning to be the editor-in-chief of *Chinese Arts & Letters*. Selection of the content for the *Library,* especially the interviews and criticisms, followed Professor Sheng Ning's suggestions. Professor Sheng Ning was formerly the editor-in-chief of *Foreign Literature Review,* the best journal in the field of foreign literature studies. On this platform, many Chinese scholars interpret and criticize foreign literature from various perspectives, facilitating the "active presence" of foreign literature in China. We hope that the *Library* will encourage scholars to criticize Chinese literature translated into English and as a part of World Literature. In other words, Professor Sheng Ning formerly focused on guiding scholars to criticize foreign literature in Chinese, but now he is focusing on guiding more scholars to criticize Chinese literature in foreign languages, including literary criticism from foreign sinologists. We hope to ensure that Chinese literature is not only effectively Going Global, but is also truly being appreciated.

A Bilingual Library of Contemporary Chinese Master Writers also aims to attract scholars' attention to the process of literary translation. As mentioned above, the translators of the *Library* are all sinologists whose mother tongue is English. At the same time, they collaborate with Chinese editors who are teachers from the School of Foreign Languages and Cultures at Nanjing Normal

University, specializing in literature or translation. The basic collaboration process involves the translator finishing the first draft and communicating with the editor whenever questions arise. After the first draft is finished, the editor proofreads it, then revises it with the translator. After the revision is completed, the editor-in-chief checks and approves the final draft. I am not a translation major, but from the time I began my job as editor at *Chinese Arts & Letters*, I was drawn to the various challenges that arose during this process. Although I knew little about translation theory, I could not wait to write an article entirely based on my own editing experience, "The Translator-Editor Collaboration in Translating Chinese Literature – Three Short Stories by Bi Feiyu as Case Studies." It has opened a new direction in my academic research, in which I have never lost interest. At present, *Chinese Arts & Letters* is setting up a Translation Process Corpus, and the materials in the translation process of *A Bilingual Library of Contemporary Chinese Master Writers* will be added to the Corpus as well. The Corpus will be open to all translation scholars to conduct studies from various perspectives and enrich the approaches to translation studies. The Translation Process Corpus showcases the communication between the translator who is a native speaker of English and the editor who is a native speaker of Chinese. They each exert their own mother tongue advantages, and interaction occurs between the two languages and cultures. They seek to make the translated text not only satisfy the target audience's reading habits and aesthetic preferences, but also convey the deepest cultural connotations of the original text. We may even imagine that if these materials crystalizing human intelligence in the translation field were "fed" in the proper way into an artificial intelligence and became deep-learning materials for AI, AI would one day translate every subtlety of the language with delicacy and beauty, breaking the bottleneck in AI translation.

Though, as mentioned earlier, the target audience of these works is relatively professional, we hope that the present *Library* will suit both refined and popular tastes and be put beside the pillows of all readers who are interested in literature. Professor Yang Haocheng once criticized young people today for being interested only in cellphones instead of books, saying, "So it is fragmented reading from the new media that college students seem to be enjoying today, and serious literature is woefully slighted or neglected, forgotten in the dust-covered shelves of the libraries, becoming the spiritual food for a minority of bookish souls." He hoped *A Bilingual Library of Contemporary Chinese Master Writers* would bring back some of "the lost lambs to the normal track of conventional paper book reading." I don't think I myself have the right to criticize young people today. Although I am not young, I read my cellphone much more frequently than I read paper books, which makes me one of "the lost lambs" criticized by Professor Yang Haocheng. But it is our hope that the *Library* will change our reading habits a little. If we plan to spend some time every day reading books, the short stories in *A Bilingual Library of Contemporary Chinese Master Writers* are an ideal starting point. As Su Tong, one of the writers introduced in Volume One of the *Library,* once said, "Short stories are like bedtime stories for adults, preferably being read beside the lamp, one piece per night. They can be tasted for three or five minutes, moving, amusing, depressing, or overwhelming the reader. If you experience these feelings, it shows that this short period of time has not been wasted. A habit like this ensures that each day will end in magnificence. How wonderful it is!" The *Library* contains wonderful short stories in both Chinese and English, which, we believe, will surely bring readers double happiness and growth.

Literary critic Wu Yiqin, academic and translator Xu Jun, and writer Su Tong have all voiced their strong support for this *Library*, each speaking from their different perspectives. These three are all towering figures in their own fields, and their opinions add to the authority of the *Library*.

This *Library* is meant to be open ended, though it is set to be developed on a five-author basis, which includes five short stories alongside a critique and an interview for each author, with slight variations in each issue. Various people have contributed their effort and lent their support to the publication of the *Library*, including our terrific translators, authors, critics, editors from *CAL* and Nanjing Normal University Press, and the Press's leadership, so you may say it's a joyful, well-orchestrated tutti.

YANG HAOCHENG

CONTENTS

CITY LIVING, COUNTRY LIVING

Translated by **Florence Woo**

Ziqing loved buying books. That in and of itself wasn't necessarily a bad thing, but over time it caused problems – the most serious of which was that there simply came to be too many books in the house. Originally, man was master over books, as they were his acquisitions. But eventually, as books grew more and more numerous, their roles reversed. Books crowded into man's living space, and man had to beg for a dwelling place in their midst. Man thus became slave to his books. In the world of books, man became more and more insignificant, more and more oppressed. So, when man wished to take back his rightful place, he must rise up against his books. How, then, did he do that? Get rid of some of them, of course, and force them to relinquish the space that originally belonged to him.

Ziqing's better half was extremely excited. She had waited many long years for this day. For all these years, she had been wishing to rid the house of all the books. In the days when Ziqing was wavering between "should I" and "should I not," she spared no effort and left no method untried to depict the books as the common enemy.

While she was normally the mistress of everything in the house, Ziqing would not yield on the book issue. Her only recourse was to present logical arguments and back them up with facts. She showed Ziqing some pieces of woollen clothing in which were little holes chewed through by worms. These worms couldn't have come from anywhere but the books. They were grey in co lor, about a centimetre long, and had slender bodies. They glided around, swift and slick, like little bolts of lightning. Camphor had no effect on them, and they seemed immune to household pesticides too – or anything else for that matter. Sometimes they even strutted across the floor in packs, as if in a show of strength. Ziqing's better half also read something in the newspapers saying that if there are too many books in a house, its inhabitants would breathe in the book-air day after day, which was bad for the health of children, making them contract respiratory illnesses more easily. Even though Ziqing didn't believe that this argument had any scientific grounds, he didn't dare risk the health of his child either.

So, in this fashion, Ziqing's better half presented more arguments for her case, and they finally produced a cumulative effect. Ziqing said, "Fine, I'll get rid of what needs getting rid of. The house is indeed getting too full."

There are many ways to get rid of books – selling them, giving them to family and friends, or even plain throwing them out. But he couldn't get himself to throw them out. Much of his collection was obtained through a great deal of perseverance and effort. For example, there was this one slim volume that Ziqing had to take the train to a small town in Zhejiang Province to dig up. There weren't very many copies of this book in print. Its topic was a bit esoteric, and the volume was not a bestseller by any means. Ziqing had not seen it anywhere else since. And now it lay among the other books to be gotten rid of. The sight of it pained Ziqing, and he ended up picking it up and putting it back on the shelf again.

His better half said, "If you keep taking this one back and taking that one back, you'll end up not getting rid of a single book at all."

Right she was. He threw it back, but the pain of parting still gnawed at his heart. These books had once been his beloved, his moral support, his anchor. To toss them out just after a few years? He could not make himself do it. His better half suggested, "If you can't bring yourself to throw them out, then sell them. At least you could get a bit of money back that way."

But old books were not worth much on the market. Selling them practically meant giving them away. While new books were listed for more and more money, old books were still sold by weight, a testimony to their worthlessness. On top of that, junk collectors were likely to short change on the weight or cheat people with non-standard scales. When Ziqing mentally pictured his old books bundled up like a pig tied up to be sent to the slaughterhouse – a pig that was muzzled and not allowed to cry – he felt wretched inside.

"Forget it," he said, "what's the point of selling them? I might as well give them away." But who would want these books? His brother-in-law said, "Nowadays you can put ten times the number of books you have in a single DVD, so what use would I have for your books?"

Then there was another fellow who was as much of a bibliophile as Ziqing was. He coveted the books, and even had space for them at home. He would have gladly taken them off Ziqing's hands but for his wife, who didn't get along with Ziqing's better half. She said, "We're not so poor that we have to take another family's rubbish."

After all that, all those books that Ziqing was so reluctant to part with were still without a new home.

Right at that time, the government launched a campaign to collect donations in the form of books and other household goods, for use in schools in disadvantaged areas. Finally Ziqing's books had somewhere to go. He bundled them up in a few large hemp cloth sacks and hired a rickshaw to carry them to the donation office. In return, he received a Certificate of Honor.

Not long after, Ziqing realized that one of his ledger books was missing. He had been in the habit of keeping a household ledger for a long time and had persisted in this habit through the years. He kept a separate volume for each year, documenting each item of household income and expense.

To be fair, bookkeeping isn't anything particularly remarkable. In many families there was a designated bookkeeper who kept the household accounts year after year. However, Ziqing's ledgers might be a bit unlike most people's. Most people's accounts were usually no more than a record of what they had bought each month and how much they had spent on it. Those who include the actual dates of the purchases were already numbered among the meticulous. Ziqing's ledgers, on the other hand, often went beyond accounting, and beyond the immediate purpose of bookkeeping. His were practically diaries. On top of writing down the items purchased, their cost, and the date of purchase, he often included details about the reason for the purchase, the background information on the item, the shopping environment, his mood at the time, how he got to the store – did he walk there? Take the bus? Take a taxi? – he recorded all that. And the weather had to be recorded clearly too. Did he get soaked in the rain? Or get too warm in the sun? Or get stuck in traffic on his way? He would put all these down as well.

He also often recorded some vignettes of things that happened during shopping, things that had nothing to do with him or his purchase. For example, one day he recorded that at 5:25 pm, he was buying fish at Dragon Market. Two crucian carp had already been weighed and thrown into his shopping basket. At that time, a sudden thunderclap exploded in the skies, scaring the fishmonger into fleeing and hiding somewhere without first collecting the payment for the fish. Ziqing remained on the spot and waited for the storm to pass. The fishmonger emerged from his hiding place. Ziqing paid him for the fish, thinking that he'd be thankful, but instead, the fishmonger said, "Aren't you a goody-two-shoes, man!" It was as if their roles had been reversed, as if Ziqing was the fishmonger, and the fishmonger was Ziqing.

Such an account had already deviated far from the original intent of bookkeeping. But Ziqing always remembered the main point of keeping his ledger. He added at the end, "Bought two crucian carp, 6 liang in weight. Price: 5 yuan per jin. Total cost: 3 yuan." Such an entry, mostly recounting non-accounting-related information, seemed to overshadow the principal function of bookkeeping. Of course, there were also other entries that were more focused on bookkeeping, such as the ones that read, "On such and such a day at such and such a time, at such and such a general store on such and such a street, bought a plastic washbasin. Blue with green lotus design. Price: 1.35 yuan."

That said, even though Ziqing's ledgers had a bit more content and were a bit more disorganized than the general household account, he mostly let his mood dictate how much or how little to write. When the mood struck him and time allowed, he might include a bit more details. When his spirits were low and time was tight, he would be a bit more terse. And sometimes he was concise to the point that no one but himself could understand what he wrote, such as "Mob: 175 yuan," which was really an entry for the amount of his mobile phone bill. No one else, not even his better half, could have guessed its meaning.

There were even entries that Ziqing himself could not decipher anymore after a few years. Take, for instance, "N. eat: 97 yuan." The phrase "N. eat," like many other words and phrases in the ledgers, should have been laid to rest after the year was over and never brought to light again. However, Ziqing was in the habit of digging up old ledgers and going over them again. He didn't have any particular purpose or reason to do so. It wasn't even out of nostalgia. He simply wanted to go over them again.

When he got to the "N. eat" entry, he paused and tried to recall the history behind that phrase. However, this little piece of history had concealed itself behind the phrase "N. eat" and refused to come out. Ziqing tried to reconstruct the logic behind the phrase. "N. eat" had the word "eat" in it, so most likely it had something to do with eating. And "N."? Perhaps it referred to dining out at a restaurant whose name started with an "N"? This ledger was from five years earlier. Ziqing pointed his memory in that direction. Which restaurants were there in town five years ago that had a name starting with "N"? And which of these would he have gone to? But this train of thought went nowhere. Restaurants came and went all the time, and it was impossible to recall what restaurants there were five years earlier. Besides, most of the time when Ziqing dined out, someone else paid for the meal. He rarely treated others to dinner. So this possibility had to be ruled out. Then, perhaps "N. eat" referred to eating out in a geographical location that started with an "N"? Could it be Nanjing, Nanxun, Nanning, or Nanchang? By the process of elimination, Ziqing ruled out this possibility as well, because he had never been to any of those places. The only N-place he had been to was a small town called Nantangwan, but he went there as a guest and his host wouldn't have let him pay for dinner anyway. Ziqing was completely stumped.

His son said, "Perhaps you didn't write clearly enough, and it's actually 'Neat'?" This was possible too. Perhaps one day he bought something that was neat, and recorded it that way? It didn't matter, though. All this was mere speculation. There were no other memories, no other physical evidence, that could reveal the true meaning of "N. eat" and where the 97 yuan was spent. Fortunately, this didn't happen frequently. All things considered, Ziqing was pretty serious and responsible with his bookkeeping.

While Ziqing's ledgers were crammed with information, they weren't very meaningful at all, nor did they have any practical use. Ziqing's original intent was probably to use bookkeeping to curb his own spending. In earlier years, when the economy was not that good, everyone tried to save money through every possible means. One of the most popular ways was through bookkeeping. In reality, though, it made nary a difference. Whatever had to go in the books went in the books, and whatever money had to be spent was spent. It wasn't as if people stopped spending a certain amount of money just because they had to record it afterward.

So after all these years, the money that had to be spent was spent, and even the money that shouldn't have been spent was spent. The stack of ledgers grew taller and taller, finally becoming a monument. They only served one use. When Ziqing had nothing better to do, on a whim, he would pick one out at random. Seeing the year on the cover of the ledger, he would let his mind drift back to that year, but he wouldn't remember exactly what that year was like. This was where the ledger came in. Its contents could help him recall some of the things that happened back then. Once he picked the 1986 volume. He first tried to remember what it was like back in 1986, but mostly he drew a blank. Then, he looked in the ledger, in which was recorded:

February' 86, Expenses:
Expenses on 3 Feb: 16.2 yuan (cooking wine: 2 yuan; pork skin: 1 yuan; chives: 0.8 yuan; snacks: 1 yuan; honey dates: 1.3 yuan; fried gluten: 0.4 yuan; mock chicken (steamed bean curd rolls): 0.8 yuan; peanuts: 0.5 yuan; washbasin: 8.4 yuan)

In the Income column, it was recorded:

9 Jan: Ziqing's monthly salary: 64 yuan.

Back in those days, his ledgers were a bit simpler, and being purely about record keeping. Nonetheless, when he looked at those records, many things that happened in the past slowly came back to him, so every time he opened up an old ledger, it was a modest, personal kind of enjoyment.

If pressed to point out a practical use for the ledgers, Ziqing would say that they could be used for some good old-fashioned education for his offspring. He could say, "See here? This is how we used to live in the old days. Look, in the old days, this is all the money we got to spend for New Year's." But Ziqing's son seemed unable to accept this kind of education. He had little concept of money, let alone any notion of saving it. Whenever Ziqing told him about the good old days, he would nod, but from the unfocused look in his eyes, Ziqing could tell that none of what he'd said sank in.

At first, Ziqing started bookkeeping because his income was low and his financial situation unstable. He used the ledger as a way to control his expenses. Then, things started looking up for him. Both he and his wife had good jobs, and their household income climbed ever higher. Even though their son was still in senior high school, he had been a great student all along and certainly one that would not become a burden on his parents. He wouldn't need a lot of money from his parents even when he went to university or study abroad in the future. On top of that, they had already bought a house, and a car as well – Ziqing's better half drove it. They were really quite well off, and there was no need for bookkeeping. Furthermore, those ledgers had no practical use anyway. All they did was accumulate through the years and take up space. Ziqing had actually played with the idea of quitting this habit, but that idea never passed the thinking stage. He just couldn't do it. The mere thought of it seemed wrong to him, let alone actually quitting. As soon as he imagined a life without ledgers, he would immediately feel an emptiness gnaw at his heart, as if he had lost something and become vulnerable. Ziqing knew that it was because old habits were hard to break. Habits were truly a powerful force.

So he kept updating his ledgers, the years kept going by, and the collection of ledgers kept growing larger. On the last day of every year, Ziqing added the past year's ledger to the ranks of the numerous ledgers of years past, organized them by year, and tucked them into the cabinet on the bottom of the bookcase. These were not for public viewing. These were for him and him alone, unlike the books which he bought. Those were placed on the shelves inside the glass doors of the bookcase, displayed for everyone to see, in a form of tacit bragging. When visitors saw them, they invariably exclaimed, "Wow! No wonder people say you're a legendary book collector. The tales are true!"

But this day, when Ziqing opened the bottom door of his bookcase, he found that a ledger had disappeared – the most recent one. They had just celebrated the New Year, and he had just started a new ledger. But last year's ledger, still warm and breathing with memories, had already gone missing. Ziqing searched the house over and racked his brain. Finally, he came to the conclusion that it was likely put among the old books and donated to disadvantaged regions.

If it was indeed donated to a disadvantaged area, that ledger would end up like the other books, in a school in some poor village. Would the school keep all the books at the school, or would they distribute them among the students? Ziqing had no way of knowing. But then, he thought, the ledger was completely useless to the children of impoverished areas. It was not a real book and was not educational at all, containing no knowledge that would benefit anyone. It was not even entertaining. No one would read it. Besides, Ziqing had his special way of bookkeeping, and his handwriting was messier than most. The country children might not be able to decipher it. And even if they could read it, the contents wouldn't mean anything to them, because they would not intersect with anything that they might have experienced in their lives. In the end, they might simply toss the ledger out.

But this was no simple matter to Ziqing. Without this ledger, life around him went on as usual, but he began to feel waves of emptiness inside, as if a part of his heart was torn out. He felt as if he had some kind of heart disease – his heart raced randomly, and his mind wouldn't focus. His better half and his friends all thought there was something wrong with his heart and told him to get a check-up at the hospital. The doctor said that his heart was fine, though the discomfort in his heart was real and not imagined. It was psychogenic. While it was not a disease of organic origins, according to the doctor, during one's middle age, emotional problems could often morph into a physical illness if not controlled and treated.

Ziqing couldn't sit still anymore. He wanted to find that lost ledger and make his heart whole again. The next day, he went to the donations office, hoping that the books were still there. Unfortunately, they had already been sent off. Luckily for him, though, the office was careful and had kept a registry of each donor's name and workplace. However, as there were many donated items – not only books, but also clothing and other household goods – the compiled registries filled half the room. The comrades at the office asked Ziqing if he had donated something important by mistake. Ziqing didn't dare to tell the truth. He knew that the staff were all busy, and if they found out that he was just looking for a family account book, they would feel that he was just making a fuss about nothing of consequence. So, Ziqing said vaguely that it was an important notebook with critical information in it.

The staff patiently sifted through the mountains of registries, and eventually found the name Jiang Ziqing. Ziqing was actually hoping that the records were more detailed and the donations itemized. If they had itemized and recorded the title of each book, Ziqing could find out right away if the ledger was among them. However, the staff told him that this was impossible. Actually, even if they hadn't told him, he would have realized the impossibility of it – when he found his own name on the registry and saw the line "donated 125 books" under the "Remarks" section, he knew that was the end of it. As for the final destination of the books, no one could tell him exactly where it was either, since it was not recorded. They did, however, know the general direction it went. That shipment of donations had gone to Gansu Province. Another point was certain – Ziqing's books, along with all the other donations, were tied up in hemp cloth sacks and stuffed into a train carriage, after which they were dragged off the train and thrown onto a lorry. They might have been transferred to yet other vehicles, but at the end they would all arrive at some school in a rural area. Their fate in this process could not be predicted or ascertained. The sacks sat in piles, one on top of another, and there was no rule or law that dictated where each sack should go. During the transfer process, chance was their fate. As for their final destination – that could only be known to the recipient. Those on this side of the process, it seemed, could never know.

In reality, though, there was a path of certainty running through all this. Even though all sorts of possibilities manifested themselves during the distribution of the sacks, each sack had its own destiny. Ziqing's sack was also on its own path of destiny, and it was not one with a dead end. If Ziqing could follow this path and keep going forward, he would end up at a place called Wang Village, in the far west of remote Gansu Province. There, a pupil at the village primary school called Wang Xiaocai received Ziqing's ledger and bring it home.

Wang Cai could read a few words, having gotten halfway through primary school. In the village, he numbered among the well-educated. Most men of his generation were illiterate. Wang Cai felt especially proud of himself, and because of that, he made his son study especially hard. He often told others, "I want Xiaocai to have an education and change the future of the old Wang family."

There had originally been no plans to distribute the donated books when they first arrived at the school. Wang Xiaocai came home that day and told his father that a lot of books had come to the school.

Wang Cai said, "If you leave them at the school, they'll just get misplaced. They might as well give them away, so everyone can take something home and read. The kids can read them, and the grown ups can too."

Someone else pointed out, "You have a grown up who could read in your family, but ours are all illiterate, so what's the point?"

But in the end, the school principal felt the same way as Wang Cai did. He said, "The donated books we got in the past have all gone missing. Instead of having that happen again, we might as well distribute them to everyone to bring home. Whoever wants to read a few more books can trade with other students." As for how the books should be distributed, the principal had that worked out too. He had a numbered tag stuck onto each book, and had the students each pick a number and take the book that corresponded to that number.

Wang Xiaocai picked the number for Ziqing's ledger. The ledger's cover was wrapped in stiff black paper, and nobody realized then that it wasn't a book – until Wang Xiaocai took it home happily and gave it to his father.

Wang Cai flipped it open. "This ain't right," he said, "This ain't no book."

Wang Cai took the ledger back to the principal. The principal said, "Even though this isn't a book, it was donated to us as one, so we distributed it among the books. You can't say you don't want it and trade it in for another one, because the school has no more books to trade with you. Maybe you can find another student whose parents are willing to trade? You're free to do with it as you wish."

But who would want a ledger? Normal books had prices printed on them – they could be a few yuan, ten yuan, or even thicker and therefore more expensive. The words in a book were printed, but ledgers were written by hand in ink, and this one didn't even have a price tag. No one wanted it. Wang Cai complained his way to the village Education Bureau, but they didn't know what to do about the matter either. In the end, they gave the one book they had kept for their own office, *On Education in Rural Primary Schools,* to placate Wang Cai, who then returned home fully satisfied.

At first Wang Cai wanted to leave the ledger with the village Education Bureau. But the comrade at the bureau said, "We don't have a use for such a thing either. We don't want it here. Just take it back with you."

Wang Cai said, "Then wouldn't I have shortchanged you? It'd be like you gave me a book for free."

The comrade at the bureau said, "All that we do here is for the good of the students. As long as the student likes it, go ahead and take it." It was only then that Wang Cai went home with both the book and the ledger.

However, neither Wang Cai nor his son could understand anything in the book from the Education Bureau. It was all about theoretical issues. Take, for example, this sentence: *The future of education in rural primary schools is dependent on first determining the problems of China's compulsory education.* But what did those problems actually refer to? Neither Wang Cai nor his son had any idea. In other words, they lacked the fundamental prerequisites for benefiting from this tome. Nonetheless, Wang Cai was not one to give up. He said to Xiaocai, "Keep it. Keep it well. The day will come when you can understand it."

Having put *On Education* aside, they were left with only the ledger. Originally, Wang Cai had felt he got a great deal, and he felt a bit sorry for having taken advantage of the village Education Bureau. Now he felt utterly dejected and believed that he had gotten a rotten deal. He ended up with a book that he couldn't read, plus a useless ledger of a townsperson. Even if you put the two together, it was still not as good of a deal as what the Xus next doors had got. What good luck their son had! He picked a travelogue by a famous author, which meant he got to follow along on his adventures and travel around the world for free. Wang Cai got upset. He brought Ziqing's ledger before him, and then he dragged Wang Xiaocai over and said, "Look at this, look at this. What kind of dastardly rotten luck do you call this?" Wang Xiaocai, knowing that he was guilty, hung his head low. From the corner of his eye, though, he took a glance at the open ledger, and saw a phrase which he could read but whose meaning was alien to him: *essential oil.*

Wang Xiaocai asked, "What does 'essential oil' mean?"

Wang Cai, stumped, looked at where those words were on the ledger. And he saw that phrase as well: *essential oil.*

And so Wang Cai started reading from where "essential oil" was written. He would never have guessed that the one look he took would ignite in him such an interest in the ledger. The contents of the volume were simply too inconceivable, too incredible to him.

First, let us, too, take a look at the contents on that page on the ledger that Wang Cai saw. This was an expense recorded one day in the year 2004:

After lunch, Yuxiu said her skin was dry, so she went to the beauty parlor to have it looked at. The beauty parlor recommended a type of essential oil. Price: 679 yuan for 7 ml. Yuxiu had a platinum card with the beauty parlor, which gave her a 30% discount, making the total 475 yuan. She took it home, opened up the box, and took a look, and it was just a bottle the size of her thumb. Apparently, you apply a few drops after washing your face, and it locks in the moisture and conditions the skin. Everyone says that these days it's easiest to swindle money from two kinds of people – women and children. I can't agree more.

Wang Cai read the entry thrice, yet he could make head nor tail of this business. He discussed this with Xiaocai, "What kind of thing do you think this is?"

"It's essential oil," replied Xiaocai.

Wang Cai said, "I can see that it's essential oil." He stuck out a thumb and continued, "It's just the size of this, and 475 yuan? It is made of money or something?"

Wang Xiaocai responded, "You and Ma couldn't farm 475 yuan out of the land working all year."

Wang Cai got upset. "Xiaocai, you saying your ma and your pa are no good?"

Wang Xiaocai replied, "No, I'm just saying that this stuff is too expensive. It's not meant for folks like us."

"Not meant for folks like us?" Wang Cai said, "Damn right. You're lucky enough to even be able to set your eyes on these words."

Wang Xiaocai said, "I want to see a 475 yuan thumb."

Wang Cai was just about to set his son straight when his wife came over to tell them it was time for dinner. She had been feeding the pigs, and when she came to announce dinner, she still had around her the apron she wore for feeding pigs, and in one hand she was holding the ladle for scooping swill. She took issue with Wang Cai and Xiaocai – she had been busy taking care of the pigs and the family on her own all this while, and they were just standing around shooting the breeze. Wang Cai said, "You wouldn't understand. We ain't shooting the breeze. We're studying how city folk live."

Wang Cai told his son to borrow a dictionary from the principal. However, the phrase "essential oil" was not listed there – they could find definitions for "essential" and "oil," but none of the definitions added up to anything meaningful.

Wang Cai swallowed and said angrily, "Enough of that! What kind of dictionary is it? It doesn't even have essential oil."

Wang Xiaocai said, "The principal told me this is this year's newest edition."

"Son of a bitch, what kind of life do city folk live?" exclaimed Wang Cai, "They have stuff that's not even in the dictionary!"

Wang Xiaocai said, "I'm gonna study hard and get into middle school, then high school, then university, and when I graduate from university I'm gonna bring you to the city."

Wang Cai asked, "How many years away is that?"

Wang Xiaocai counted on his fingers, and replied, "I'm in fifth grade this year, so there are eleven years to go."

Wang Cai said, "I've got to wait eleven years? The essential oil's gonna be rancid by then!"

"Then I'll study even harder and skip grades," offered Wang Xiaocai.

"Skip grades? With what you've got?" Wang Cai retorted, "If you can skip grades, I am university material!"

Actually, Wang Cai had placed great hope on Xiaocai all along. At the very least, Wang Xiaocai had made it to fifth grade without showing any signs that the hope was misplaced, and Wang Cai was very proud of his son. However, the appearance of this ledger put his thoughts in disarray. He looked at the boy standing in front of him, face covered with snot. He suddenly thought, "I can't count on this kid. I can only count on myself."

Wang Cai decided to take his family to go to live in the city, becoming a "migrant worker," in today's terms. The only difference was that in most other families, the man moved to the city first, and only after making a decent living there would he come back to bring his wife and children to the city. There were others who settled in nicely in the city and never came back, some even getting themselves a new wife and new children in the city. But there were others who couldn't make it and returned home for good. But Wang Cai was different. He wasn't going out there to test the waters. He left expressly to live in the city, to become city folk.

As unbelievable as it sounds, it was all because of the words "essential oil" in the ledger. Wang Cai thought to himself, "Son of a bitch, I've lived half my life for nothing. I don't even know what 'essential oil' is. I have to go to the city to see this 'essential oil' for myself."

Wang Cai's wife objected to Wang Cai's decision. She thought Wang Cai had gone mad. However, in the country, wives had no say over anything their men decided on. Even if her man wasn't taking her into the city, but instead into prison or even into Hell, she could not have protested. But Wang Xiaocai remained ambivalent. He could only feel confusion and bewilderment. In the end, he managed to let out a little mouse-like squeak, "I don't wanna go. I don't wanna go." But Wang Cai wouldn't listen to him. Wang Xiaocai was not in a position to speak.

Wang Cai left as soon as he made up his mind. The next day, a large padlock was hung at his front door with a note reading, "I owe so-and-so 3 yuan, and so-and-so 5 yuan, and I will honor that. When I've made my fortune and return, I will repay double these amounts in full. As for those who owe me, I'll let bye gones be bye gones, as my parting gift to my fellow villagers."

As Wang Cai pasted the note on his door, Wang Xiaocai asked, "What does 'double these amounts in full' mean?"

Wang Cai replied, "'In full' means you pay the original amount you owe, and 'double' means you pay more than the original amount, twice as much."

Wang Xiaocai continued to ask, "Then does it mean you'll repay just the original amount or twice that?"

Wang Cai answered, "You are too young to understand. But if you read more of that ledger, you'll eventually get it."

Actually, Wang Xiaocai should have picked out other errors that his father made, such as writing "bygones" as "bye gones." But Wang Xiaocai was not at that good either. He had never even heard of the phrase "let bygones be bygones."

Apart from their clothes, Wang Cai's family didn't bring anything else with them – not that there was anything else in their house. The only exception was Ziqing's ledger, which Wang Cai felt obliged to carry on his person, since he had to read it every day. He read it slowly, as some words in the book were unfamiliar to him. There were also some phrases with words that he did recognize, but whose meaning eluded him. Take "essential oil" for example – Wang Cai still hadn't figured out what that could be.

While on the bus, Wang Cai got to this passage:

Sunday. It's almost the New Year. People on the streets were walking hurriedly but in good spirits, and joy was evident on their faces. In the afternoon I went to the Flower and Bird Market. Even though it was frigid outside, the place was quite crowded. Among the plethora of wares, it was the phalaenopsis orchid alone that caught my eye. The asking price was 800 yuan, but I talked them down to 600. I brought it home, and both Yuxiu and Xiaodong loved it. When I placed it on the coffee table next to the sofa in the living room, it looked like a couple of butterflies flittering about, bringing vitality into the house with their dancing.

After a while, Wang Cai fell asleep in the bus. He had a dream, in which a butterfly said to him, "Wang Cai, Wang Cai, get up!"

Wang Cai panicked, "Butterflies can't talk. You can't be a butterfly!"

The butterfly laughed, and Wang Cai woke up in a fright. For a long while after waking up, his heart was still wildly pitter-pattering. Eventually, he couldn't help but ask his son, "Hey, can butterflies talk?"

Wang Xiaocai thought for a bit and replied, "Never heard of it."

Just then, their bus pulled into a little train station. Here, they had to buy train tickets, then take the train south, then east, then south, then east again to a city far, far away. There were many cities in China, and how would Wang Cai – who had never left his home village, and who couldn't tell east from west – know which city he wanted to go to? Needless to say, it was Ziqing's ledger that gave him guidance. On the cover of Ziqing's ledger he not only put down the year, but also the name of the city where he lived, written in neat handwriting. He wrote, "By Ziqing in the City of..., in the Year of..."

The trains that stopped at the little train station were slow trains, and they didn't come frequently at all. While waiting for their train, Wang Cai looked at the ledger again, trying to see if the author had written anything about taking the train. Despite flipping through the volume from cover to cover, he found nothing. In the end, Wang Cai slapped himself on the mouth and said, "You moron! He's city folk. Why would he take the train? Only country folk have to take the train to the city."

Actually, Ziqing did end up making a trip out to Gansu. Going the opposite direction from Wang Cai's family, he first took the train, then the bus, then a motor scooter, then a donkey cart, and finally in the western reaches of Gansu Province he found Wang Village, and there he found the Wang Village Primary School.

There he found out that his ledger had indeed arrived at the school and was given to a student named Wang Xiaocai. And he learned that Wang Xiaocai's parents took issue with that and came to the school to protest, and that in the end they received another book from the village Education Bureau as compensation.

Ziqing's own journey, while less than straightforward, was an informative one, but even so, he had come too late. Wang Xiaocai's father had already brought their whole family to the city. The bus that they took to get to the train station and the bus that Ziqing took to get to the village passed each other. At that moment, Wang Cai was looking at Ziqing's ledger, and Ziqing was thinking about what to write in his ledger that day. However, whatever he thought about on the bus and what ended up being written were two completely different things, because when he was on the bus, he had not arrived at Wang Village yet.

That evening, under the dim light in the little guesthouse, Ziqing wrote down the following:

It's early spring in a village in the West, a vast, open place, where everything is so serene and remote. As soon as I set foot on this land, I was able to liberate my mind from the clamor and confusion of the city and enjoy this precious tranquility in peace. When I arrived at the Wang Village Primary School, the principal wasn't there. He was in court standing trial. The school had incurred an amount for emergency repairs that he was unable to pay, and the school had been in arrears. This is his fourth year as principal and his seventh time standing trial.

Around lunch time, he came back. He said to me grinning, 'Comrade Jiang, I'm sorry to keep you waiting.' He didn't look like someone who had just stood trial. He was unruffled – probably out of helplessness, and also out of sheer poverty. I said, 'Sir, I heard that you were owing construction costs.' He said, 'In the past, our school received education subsidies, and we held out by spending on deficit. But the subsidies have since been cancelled, and we can't hold out anymore.' I said, 'Then what can you do?' He said, 'Well, we still have to hold out. The school has to keep running, and the students have to go to school. The school cannot close down. Don't you agree, Comrade Jiang?' This kind of calm acceptance in the face of abject poverty is a rare sight in modern cities that are undergoing such dramatic changes.

Today's expenses: Guesthouse, 3 yuan; motor scooter fare outgoing, 5 yuan (original offered price 2 yuan); donkey cart returning, 5 yuan (original offered price 1 yuan). Breakfast, 20 cents. Two corn cakes, ate one and gave one to the owner of the scooter. Dinner, 50 cents. Three liang of plain noodles. Lunch, 50 cents. The principal said I need not pay and it was on him, but I insisted on paying anyway. Wanted to pay a bit more but he firmly refused to take it. Ate it along with the students. Plain rice with cabbage, with cabbage soup on the side. Wang Xiaocai normally eats here too, but today he is gone. I wonder where he had lunch today and what he ate.

At long last, Ziqing saw that note on the front door of Wang Xiaocai's house. The handwriting was crooked and uneven, so Ziqing assumed that it was the work of the primary school student who received his ledger. He would not have guessed that it was the handiwork of the schoolboy's father. Wang Xiaocai was in fifth grade, but his father, Wang Cai, only had a fourth grade education. Normally, if any writing had to be done at home, it fell to Xiaocai. However, this time, Wang Cai apparently felt that his son was incapable of handling the gravity of the task, and so he took charge of it himself.

Ziqing never found his lost ledger. However, his feeling of loss dissipated over the course of this arduous journey. The moment he stood before the little mud hut and saw the words "let bye gones be bye gones," he suddenly cheered up. All the knots and gnarls in his heart were gone. His ledger was gone forever, but so were his restless, anxious days.

When Ziqing returned home from the Great Northwest, he saw that a migrant farmer family had moved into the garage next door. Every house in Ziqing's neighborhood had a garage. Some families never bought their own car. Some of them had access to a company car which was only used for pick-ups and drop-offs, and which was never parked at home, leaving their garage free. Some families rented out their garages for migrant worker families to live in.

That migrant family was none other than Wang Cai's. As he worked as a junk collector, he got to know the inhabitants of the neighborhood well in a short time.

The days were getting hotter. One day, Ziqing passed by the front of the garage, and saw that Wang Cai and his wife were there under the sun, tying the junk they had bought into bundles. They were covered in sweat, and the rags on their backs were soaked through. One of the neighborhood dogs was barking furiously at them. The dog's owner came to lead it away, scolding.

Wang Cai said, "Don't scold it. It's not like it understands."

The dog owner said, "Stupid son of a bitch!"

Wang Cai said, "It's fine. It's just because it doesn't know us well. Once it gets used to us, it won't bark anymore. Dogs are all like that."

At dusk, Ziqing walked by again. He saw that the garage they lived in was packed to the rafters with their wares, and not a waft of outside breeze got in. Ziqing felt compelled to ask, "Sir, it must be hot inside at night, since you don't have windows in the garage?"

Wang Cai answered, "Not at all." He reached out and tugged on a cord. A ceiling fan started to spin, making swooshing noises. Wang Cai continued, "Guess how much this cost me?"

Ziqing couldn't guess correctly. Wang Cai laughed and said, "I'll tell you. I found this on the streets. City living is definitely better than country living – never imagined you could scrounge electric fans just off the streets!"

Ziqing wanted to say something, but could utter no word.

Wang Cai continued, "It's so great here in the city. If we hadn't come here, we'd never know how nice it is to live in the city. In the vegetable market, you can pick up all sorts of greens and not pay a cent for them."

Wang Cai's wife, though normally reticent, suddenly added, "I've picked up a fish once, and a live one at that! There ain't nothing wrong with it except it's a bit small, and so the fishmonger threw it out."

Ziqing said, "But back in the country you could have grown your own greens."

Wang Cai replied, "Back where we're from, it's just sand and rocks everywhere, and there ain't no water neither. We couldn't grow no grain or vegetables. And even if we had vegetables, we wouldn't have any oil to cook them with anyway."

From their accent Ziqing fathomed that they were from the west, but he didn't ask what their hometown was. All he could think of was, "People used to say, 'Gold dish or silver dish, it cannot compare to your own dog's dish.' But nowadays people don't think like that anymore. There are more and more people leaving their hometowns now."

When Wang Cai talked to Ziqing, he tried to speak in standard Mandarin as much as possible. Even though he had an accent, at least others could get the gist of his meaning. If they spoke in their local dialect, Ziqing would have no way of understanding anything. Later on, however, they talked among themselves in their own dialect. And when Wang Xiaocai came home from the School for the Children of Migrant Workers, Wang Cai asked him, "Did you go look at the dictionary at school like I told you to?"

Wang Xiaocai replied, "I did! The dictionary at school is this big and this thick. I couldn't even pick it up."

Wang Cai said, "So what's a phalaenopsis orchid?"

Wang Xiaocai replied, "It's a kind of flower."

Wang Cai said, "Son of a bitch, you can sell a flower for that much money? City living is definitely better than country living!"

Ziqing didn't understand what that was about, but he could sense their satisfaction with life. Later on, they also talked about his ledger. They were grateful to the ledger for changing their lives, allowing them to move from the deprived countryside to the prosperous city, where everything was available. Ziqing didn't understand that either, nor did he know that, every evening, when he had some time to himself, Wang Cai would read the ledger. Not only did Wang Cai read Ziqing's ledger, but he got into the habit of keeping his own records too. This day, he wrote, "Received 35 jin of old books, paid 50 cents per jin, sold for 90 cents a jin at the recycling center. Net profit for this transaction was 40 cents × 35 jin, or 14 yuan. City living is definitely better than country living. The old books were sold to me by the man with the glasses living upstairs. They say he's got more books at home than he has space for, so he'll have more to sell for sure. I should develop a good relationship with him. Next time I'll tip the scale a bit more for him."

One Sunday, Wang Xiaocai went out for a walk with his father. They passed by a beauty par lor. In the display window, they finally saw their first essential oil. Upon spotting it, Wang Xiaocai shouted out in delight, "Oh! Oh! This one is cheap! The price went down! This 10 ml bottle is just 407 yuan."

Wang Cai snapped, "What would you know? It's a different brand, so the price is different. Cheap, my ass. This kind of thing only ever gets more and more expensive. Xiaocai, lemme tell you, you're just country folk, so shut up if you don't know what you're talking about."

YING YANG ALLEY

Translated by **Helen Wang**

The sun was shining warmly on the walls and on the ground, and three old ladies were in the yard enjoying the sunshine. As their faces turned a rosy pink, a small child ran in, saying, "Mrs Tang, you've got a visitor."

"A visitor for me?" The old woman said. "Now who could that be?"

"I don't know," said the child. "It's an old man."

One of the ladies giggled with a toothless grin, like a child.

The old man had already come inside. He was wearing a peaked cap, like a young man, and he stood in front of the old ladies, not quite sure what to do with his hands and feet. He squinted in the sunlight.

The ladies cast their somewhat blurry eyes at his face. He blushed a little.

"I'm looking for Mr Huang's wife," he said. "She's called Tang. Tang's her family name."

One of the ladies laughed.

Mrs Tang felt a bit awkward too. "You're looking for me?" she said. "My name's Tang."

"Oh," the old man said happily, "then I've found you. You must be Mr Huang's wife."

Mrs Tang didn't recognize him.

"Where are you from?" she asked.

"Me?" said the old man. "I came from the train station."

"You just got off the train?"

"Yes." He pulled a name-card out of his pocket, and handed it to Mrs Tang, saying," Here's my name-card. My name's Mai."

"Oh." Mrs Tang looked at the name-card, but she couldn't see the characters clearly. "I'll go and fetch my glasses," she said. "Take a seat inside."

"My? Are there people called My?" asked one of the ladies.

The old man followed Mrs Tang inside the house.

"It's going to snow," said one of the ladies.

"Do you think so? When the sun is so lovely?" asked the other lady.

"Yes," said the other, "it always snows in winter."

Mrs Tang put on her glasses. She read the old man's name. "I'm afraid I don't remember who you are." She was quite apologetic. "I'm old now, and my memory's not so good."

"You don't know me," said the old man. "We've never met, and you wouldn't know my name."

"Oh," said Mrs Tang. "You said you just got off the train. Where have you come from?"

"From the south."

"Where are you going?"

"To the north."

"Do you mean Beijing?" said Mrs Tang.

"Yes, Beijing. I'm on a work trip to Beijing. I've got some work to do there, so I took the train."

"When I was young, I moved to Beijing with my husband," said Mrs Tang. "Beijing's a big place, and it doesn't get too cold in winter."

"I know," said the man, "I know that the two of you lived in Beijing."

At first Mrs Tang was a bit bewildered, then she worked it out. "Ah, you must have known our Mr Huang back then," she said.

"I didn't know him," said old man. "Actually, I never met him. I admired him greatly, but our paths never crossed."

"He's been gone a long time," said Mrs Tang. "Over forty years now."

"I know."

"You say you're taking the train to Beijing," said Mrs Tang." "So you interrupted your journey to come here?"

"Yes."

"You got off the train specially to come and visit me?" she asked, a little suspiciously.

"I had to find out your address first," said the man. "I'd known for a long time that you'd gone back home, but I never knew where that was. I had to make some enquiries."

"There are lots of little streets here. It's not easy to find," said Mrs Tang, "not easy at all."

"It wasn't so difficult," said the man. "Lots of people knew of Ying Yang Alley, and could remember where Mr Huang lived."

"Have some tea," She pushed a teacup in front of him. "Have some tea."

"This looks like Biluochun, gunpowder tea," he said. "I don't know very much about tea. I don't really understand it. I can't tell what's good and what's not."

"I do know about tea," she replied. "I'm very particular about tea. I can tell by looking whether it's good or not."

"I know," said the man. "You knew a lot about tea when you were young too."

She smiled, a bit embarrassed. "It's still the same, I only drink good tea," she said. "If it's not good, I won't drink it."

There was a noise in the yard. Mrs Tang went out to see what it was, then came back inside and said, "It's a beggar."

"Oh," said the man. "This courtyard house of yours must be a hundred years old."

"More or less a hundred," she replied.

"I read about it in a book," he said. "It was in a book of essays that I couldn't put down."

"So you got off the train specially to come and visit me," said Mrs Tang.

"But the street is not called Ying Yang Alley in that book. And it took me a while to work it out."

"It used to be called Yin-Yang Alley," she said.

They both laughed. "Yin-Yang, it's quite an unusual name for an alley," said the man.

"Then the name was changed and it became Ying Yang Alley," said Mrs Tang. "It sounds similar when you say it, but the written characters are completely different."

The small child ran in again. "Mrs Tang, the rag-and-bone man is here. He wants to know if you have any newspapers to sell."

"Not today," she said. "Tell him to come another time. I've got a visitor today."

The child looked at the old man. "You're a visitor," the child said, then ran out again.

The old man took a sip of tea.

"The tea's gone cold," said Mrs Tang. "Let me pour a bit out and fill it up again, so it will be hot."

"There's no need," said the old man.

"Lukewarm tea's not nice. Tea should be drunk boiling hot. That's when it tastes best," said Mrs Tang. "You got off the train specially to come and visit me."

"You used to go to Zhenhua Girls' School in Shanghai. I was at Wutong School next door," said the old man, "just the other side of the wall."

"Wutong," said the old lady. "Wutong was a very good school, but they didn't take girls in those days."

"That's why you didn't know me," said the old man, "but I knew you. You were the school's beauty queen. All the boys knew you. We would hang around the gates of Zhenhua Girls' School, hoping to see you."

She was a bit embarrassed. "Is that so?" she said. "I wasn't aware of it."

"That's how it was," said the old man. "I've wanted to see you for ages, but I never had the chance. When all the girls came out of school, I didn't know which one was you."

"Is that so?" She blushed a little. "It was such a long time ago."

"It was a long time ago," said the old man, "a very long time ago."

"Where did you go afterwards?" she asked.

"Afterwards I went to many places," he replied. "I learned that you and Mr Huang had tied the knot. We all knew Mr Huang was a gifted young man. It was a perfect match, truly, 'wit and beauty.'"

"Afterwards, my husband opened a school," said Mrs Tang, "and I was his assistant."

"I know," said the old man. "Actually, it was more than 'wit and beauty.' You yourself were a gifted young woman. You had brains as well as beauty."

She smiled, and he smiled too. For a while neither of them said anything. Noises from the yard and from the street came and went, and the atmosphere in the room seemed to open.

"Have some tea," said Mrs Tang.

"I'm fine," said the old man.

"Such a long time ago," she said.

"Such a long time ago," he said. "I've held this wish in my heart all these years. That's why I'm here. Nothing was going to stop me getting off the train specially to come and visit you."

"You got off the train. That means you'll have to catch another one," she said. "Is it a lot of trouble to change trains?"

"It's no trouble."

"You'll have to buy a ticket for the onward journey," she said.

"Yes, they've already bought it for me," he replied.

"They?"

"The two colleagues who are going to Beijing with me."

"They got off with you?"

"Yes."

"They had to buy tickets for the onward journey too?"

"Yes."

"Oh," she said.

"I'm so happy," said the old man.

"I'm happy too," she replied.

"Mrs Tang!" a voice called from outside, then hurried in.

"What is it, Mrs Lin?" asked Mrs Tang.

"You've got a visitor," said Mrs Lin. "Would you like me to buy you something for dinner?"

"There's no need," said the old man.

"But you must stay and eat," said Mrs Lin.

"They're waiting for me at the station," said the old man. "I'd better say goodbye."

The old man got up. Mrs Tang got up too. The old man said, "I'd better say goodbye."

"You're leaving? But you must stay!" said Mrs Lin.

"Thank you," said the old man, "but I have to go."

Mrs Tang saw him off at the door. The old man glanced back at the yard. "It's almost exactly as I imagined," he said.

"Is that so?"

"Yes," said the old man. "I always imagined you would live in a place like this."

"Is that so?"

"Yes," said the old man. "I always imagined you like this."

A tricycle came along. "Mrs Tang, is this your visitor?" asked the driver.

"Yes."

"Does he need a trike?"

"Yes."

"Where to?"

"The train station."

"Oh," said the driver, "you're taking the train. Where are you going?"

"To Beijing."

"Oh, that's a long way."

The old man got into the tricycle, looked back at Mrs Tang and waved. "I'm going now," he said.

She nodded, and the tricycle headed off into the distance.

Mrs Tang went back inside.

"Who was he?" everyone asked.

"An old friend."

"Where from?"

"He's a friend from the past," she said.

"What's his name?"

"He's called..." she had to think for a moment. "He's called Mai."

"My?" said one of the old ladies. "Are there people called My?"

BORN IN AN UNKNOWN HOUR

Translated by **Shelly Bryant**

An elderly comrade who had retired from the work unit passed away. This was a normal occurrence – when a person is old, he will die. But there was something slightly different about this situation. Two comrades in the veteran cadre's office were not currently on duty. Ding was on maternity leave, and Jin was overseas visiting his daughter, so there was no one in the work unit to attend to the matter. That wouldn't do, so the unit chief divided up the duties between the various departments, with some of the staff going to the home of the old comrade to help with funeral preparations and others contacting the funeral parlor for the burial service where people could pay their last respects to the deceased. The staff member in charge of paperwork in the work unit, Liu Yan, was assigned the task of writing the old comrade's obituary. The task was not heavy or difficult, since most of the content was already there. It only required a visit to the HR office to check the details in the file there, then all he had to do was piece together the comrade's experiences in the obituary. For Liu, whose bread and butter was dealing with paperwork, this was nothing more than preparing a quick bite.

Although the comrade had been retired for over twenty years before Liu had started at the work unit, Liu's mind always worked quickly, like a vehicle moving smoothly along a well-laid highway. He only stood in front of the archive cabinets of the HR office for a few minutes, flipped through a few pages, and his thoughts were already organized, the comrade's lifetime of experiences formulating in his mind. A variety of forms had accumulated in the old man's file over the years and, when put together, they told the whole life story of the deceased comrade. Some of the forms had been prepared by the comrade himself, and others had been filled up on his behalf by his work units or other people. The information and formalities were basically the same. Where there were discrepancies, they did not amount to much. For instance, one form said he had entered the work unit in June in a certain year, while another said it was July of the same year. The nature of the work was the same on the two forms. It was only the starting date that was off by a month. No one had bothered to correct it since, at the end of the day, it was not a big deal.

At first, this just passed unnoticed. Liu had outlined the obituary in his mind and, based on his usual writing speed, thought it would take him about half an hour to put it down on paper. When he started to take the old comrade's file back to the archives, he shot a fleeting glance at the form on the top of the pile, with the old comrade's name listed as Zhang Xiaosheng (张萧生). Liu felt it a little unfamiliar. Looking at another form beneath the top, he noticed that the name was written with a different character at the end – 声 instead of 生. The two words were pronounced exactly the same, but represented by different characters. As he flipped through the rest of the forms, he found a total of three variations of the written name, with the third reading Zhang Xiaosen (张萧森). Liu asked one of the staff members in the HR office about it. Being quite experienced, the fellow felt it was nothing out of the ordinary. It was inevitable that there would be occasional glitches, and he just needed to go by the name filled in by the old comrade himself. Liu shuffled through the file to find a form written in the old comrade's own hand, took that version of the name, and completed the obituary.

When the obituary was in the hands of the old comrade's widow, she was clearly displeased, even at first glance. The old man's widow said, "The work unit is so sloppy, writing the old man's name wrong. It's 'shen' (身), not 'sheng' (声)."

Liu said, "I checked personally in his file. He filled in the form himself."

The woman said, "How could that be? Are you saying he didn't know how to write his own name?"

Liu replied, "There were several different versions of the name in his file, so I wasn't sure which was correct."

The woman replied, "But I'm sure. We're family! I have lived with this name every day for many years. Do you think I'm mistaken?"

Liu felt he was in a tight spot. The old comrade's widow was telling him the name was "shen," a completely new version. But it wasn't anywhere in the archive, so how could he just accept her story?

He took the obituary back and consulted the HR office. The staff there said, "This won't work. Everything should go by what is found in the archives. You can't just assign a name arbitrarily. That would be a big joke."

Liu said, "But I can't confirm it based on the archive, because there are three different versions of his name there."

The staff said, "I told you earlier what to do, so why are you coming around with the same problem?"

Liu's normally high-speed mind seemed to hit a roadblock. He scratched his head and said, "Coming around? I'm not sure how I came around to the same problem. No wonder everyone says working with bureaucracy is so difficult. You wind around and around, making everything so complicated."

The HR staff smiled and said, "If you're really worried, go back to his previous work unit, and that should clear it up. He worked there for decades before transferring to us. He was here for just a couple of years, and then he retired. Maybe the information there is more reliable."

Liu got a letter of introduction and went to the comrade's previous work unit. It was a female comrade who attended to him. This woman looked at the letter and, seemingly at a loss, asked, "What do you want?"

Liu laid out the problem as simply as he could. The woman cried, "Oh, I'm new here too, so I'm not very familiar with things yet. Let me make a phone call and ask."

When she had dialed, she said, "There's someone here from some work unit enquiring about Mr Zhang's situation. Which Mr Zhang?" She looked at the introductory letter from Liu Yan and said, "He's Zhang Xiaosheng – no, the other 'sheng.' But, actually, that's the problem. We're not sure if it's 'sheng,' 'shen,' 'seng,' or 'sen,' nor which character it should be. Maybe–" She looked at Liu Yan, who quickly wrote out the various characters he had encountered so far. The woman looked, then read off the options before saying, "What? What? OK... OK... got it. So, that's what's wrong."

She put the phone down, her expression a mixture of puzzlement and displeasure. She looked at Liu Yan and said, "What do you want to bring up this old comrade for? Mr Zhang died many years ago. Why are you writing his obituary now?"

Shocked, Liu Yan said, "How is that possible? Mr Zhang died the day before yesterday. Our department head went personally to the hospital to offer his condolences."

The woman looked at him dubiously, but finally seemed to believe him. She said, "Hu must have made a mistake."

He expected her to make another phone call to enquire but, instead, she began muttering to herself, *When everyone is talking nonsense, who can I trust? I have to depend on myself. I'll look for information myself and see what I can turn up.* But after a bit of rummaging and shuffling through the files, she realized that there was a problem. She stopped and said, "Aiyah, this won't work. Mr Zhang was transferred to your department. How would his files still be here?"

Liu said, "I didn't come here to find more records. I just came to find out the correct way to write his name."

The woman said, "Oh, then I'll find some people you can ask."

Leaving Liu Yan alone in her office, she went out. That seemed a bit careless. Liu Yan did not like being left alone in a stranger's office. What if something happened? He quickly got up and followed her out. He saw the woman entering an office across the corridor, calling loudly, "Do any of you know Zhang Xiaosheng?"

Everyone in the other office was burying themselves in work. At her loud question, they were dazed for a while before someone said, "I knew Zhang Xiaosheng. He's an old comrade. What do you need?"

The woman said, "Yes, he's gone now. We're not sure how to write his name. His new work unit wants to know whether it was 'sheng,' 'shen,''seng,' or 'sen,' and which character."

Another said, "Hey, if he's already gone, why all the bother for such details? But anyway, it's not 'sheng'" – and he added yet another possibility to their list of characters, a word meaning "promotion." – "Can someone dead still hope for a promotion?"

The woman snapped, "Don't be silly. The fellow from his new unit is waiting for an answer now."

There was a commotion as everyone spoke at once. There were all sorts of options raised, but none had any real grounds on which to treat it as trustworthy, being based merely on speculation. Before long, many new potential characters had been offered for the last word in the old comrade's name. Fed up, the woman in charge said, "Aiyah! Everyone's just spouting nonsense. He just came in here to ask a simple question, and all you can do is muddy the waters further."

Liu Yan felt the group had been a bit disrespectful to the deceased. The way they spoke so lightly, one wouldn't think an old comrade had just passed away, but that he was sitting right there in the office, the object of their barbs and banter.

At the woman's protest, they stopped chattering. After a moment had passed in silence, one person suddenly said, "Are you talking about Mr Zhang? Zhang Xiaosheng? I saw him at the park yesterday – how can you say he passed away the day before?"

Surprised, the woman said, "Maybe you saw your own ghost!"

Another woman stifled a laugh, quickly covering her mouth. The person who spoke before thought for quite a long time before he said in haste, "Oh! I take it back! I was mistaken. He wasn't the one I saw yesterday. That was Mr Li. Sorry."

Everyone told him not to feel bad, and that there was nothing to apologize for. It had been a long time, many years since the fellow retired, in fact. And it wasn't like they met often, so it would be easy to make a mistake. Things like that just happened sometimes.

Not wishing to hear anymore, Liu quietly backed out, but the woman in charge had a sharp eye. She followed him and said, "Hey! Where are you going? We haven't done with it yet. If you have to leave, at least don't go and report that we have a bad attitude!"

Liu Yan answered as politely as he could, "Don't worry. It's the same in our unit."

Liu made his way back to the old comrade's home, where he saw the fellow's portrait hanging on the wall. Feeling a surge of compassion, he said to the widow, "We'll use 'shen,' like you said."

She replied, "Of course you will. After all, I'm right. If I'm mistaken, who could possibly be correct?"

Liu took out the draft of the obituary, intending to make the amendment. Just then, someone came into the room, objecting loudly. It was the old man's daughter. She disagreed. "Ma," she said, "you're mistaken. My father's name was Zheng Xiaosheng (张萧升)."

Enraged, her mother took their hukou, the household registration booklet, out of a drawer. Pointing, she said, "Look here."

Liu looked and saw that it said, "Zhang Xiaoshen," without a doubt, just as the woman had said. He felt the dispute could be settled, finally, but the daughter produced another hukou, saying, "This is the family's old hukou."

The two booklets were not the same. One had a grey cardboard cover, the other a red plastic one. At one glance, he could tell that they were legacies from two different eras. But what was strange was that the widow held the newer hukou, while the daughter had the old one.

Liu said, "When you made the new hukou, you didn't return the old one?"

The daughter replied, "We didn't make a new one. We split his residence. I live in the old house, so I have the old booklet. In it, my father is clearly named Zhang Xiaosheng."

The old woman was furious. She said, "Anyway, no matter what you say, the old man was my old man. No one can be more certain about this than I am."

Seeing that her mother was being unreasonable, the daughter turned tough herself and said, "Surely you didn't personally witness my grandparents naming him?"

The old woman said, "Well, we ate from the same pot for some sixty years, so I might as well have been there to see it with my own eyes."

The daughter shot back, "Even if you saw it with your own eyes, it has been over eighty years now. Maybe your mind is muddled!"

The old woman turned and went back into the room in a huff, slamming the door behind her.

At an impasse with the task at hand, Liu Yan was uncertain what to do next. Beside him, the daughter smiled and said, "Well, comrade, don't frown. It's not that difficult. You can just write what my mother said."

Liu Yan replied, "Is it fine with you? You won't be angry?"

The daughter said, "Why so much anger? I just can't stand my mother. She thinks she's always right. I just want to fight with her a little. Anyway, the fight is over. Whether my father was Zhang Xiaoshen or Zhang Xiaosheng, he isn't here now, so what's the point worrying about it?"

Pleased to have come to a truce, Liu was about to modify the name. Just then, the old woman burst into the room, carrying several papers and crying, "I don't understand!"

Enraged at her daughter, the woman had gone into the bedroom to search for evidence. She had turned up several documents, including the old man's identity card, work permit, health permit, retirement card, senior citizen card, and travel documents, but the names on these documents were not uniform. The woman said furiously, "How could this happen? What's wrong with these people? It's outrageous!"

Her daughter advised, "Ma, how can you blame others? You didn't pay attention or take note yourself. If you had, you could have corrected the errors earlier."

The old woman snapped, "Correct? With so many different names, which one do I change it to?"

The younger woman laughed and said, "Just pick the one you thought it should be."

This seemed to quell the old woman's anger. Watching Liu modify Mr Zhang's name to Xiaoshen in the obituary, she seemed satisfied that the matter was complete.

Liu went back to the work unit and told everyone about his experience. Hearing it, one colleague said, "Liu Yan, you took the task too seriously. The old fellow's not around anymore. Do you really need to be so meticulous?"

Another said, "Why all the trouble, do you really think it will bring comfort to Mr Zhang?"

Another added, "You may end up comforting the wrong Mr Zhang. That would be embarrassing!"

Liu wanted to say something in his own defense but, after thinking for a long while, he could not come up with a single word, not knowing how to defend and for whom.

When he went home that evening, Liu took out a few of his own important documents and felt reassured after he found that the names on all these papers were uniform in print. Surprised, his wife asked what he was doing.

"I'm looking at my name," he replied.

Even more surprised by his answer, she said, "What's to look at? Your name followed you from the time you were born. Surely you don't think it just changed one day?"

Feeling comforted, Liu did not reply.

A few days later, the Qing Ming Festival rolled around, so Liu Yan took his wife and daughter to his hometown to visit the ancestral graves. On the way, they came across an old villager grinning at them from ear to ear. He did not recognize the fellow, but seeing his toothless grin, Liu felt a rush of warm affection for him. At the same time, he felt a little awkward, and so just smiled, nodded, and tried to shuffle past. Unexpectedly, the villager blocked his path and said warmly, "Hey, Bunny, you're back."

His daughter tittered and parroted, "Hey, Bunny! Hey, Bunny!" The more she thought about it, the harder she laughed, until her stomach ached and she doubled over with it.

Caught off guard, Liu said to the old man, "Uncle, I think you've got the wrong person. I'm not Bunny."

The man said, "Who says you're not Bunny? You are, and you have been since you were little."

Liu said, "I was the fourth child in my family, so my nickname was always Fourth Boy."

The old man said, "It's not your nickname. You were born in the year of the rabbit, so we always called you Bunny."

"Aha!" cried Liu Yan. "Then you are mistaken. I wasn't born in the year of the rabbit, but of the snake."

Seeing him speak so convincingly, the old man hesitated. After staring at Liu's face for a moment, he said, "You're the fourth child in the Liu family?"

"That's right."

The old man clapped his hands. "Then, I'm right. It's you! Bunny. When you were small, that's what we called you."

Liu said, "Then why don't I remember it?"

The old man looked surprised, and said, "You people become city dwellers, and you have to change your zodiac sign too?"

Liu said, "I didn't change anything. I was indeed born in the year of the snake."

The old man did not seem to bother enough to argue with Liu. Calling two other elderly villagers over, he asked, "The fourth kid in the Liu family – what year was he born?"

The two villagers glanced at Liu Yan. One said, "Fourth kid in the Liu family... he was born in the year of the dog. We called him Puppy."

The other said, "No! It was the year of the monkey."

Liu sighed. "So you called him Little Monkey?"

His wife and daughter were convulsed with laughter. "Stop it," they said. "My stomach hurts from laughing so much."

Not knowing what they were laughing at, one of the old villagers said, "City life must be good. Look how happy they are."

Not wanting to fuss over this with the old villagers, Liu left, making his way first to the ancestral grave, then hurrying to his oldest brother's house. Of the four brothers, only the oldest remained living in the countryside. The two of them went to the dinner table, where they went through the ritual of sprinkling wine on the floor as an offering to their deceased parents before drinking a cup themselves. His oldest brother was reserved, not saying much as he drank. Liu Yan spoke up on behalf of his other two brothers, saying, "They meant to come back, but they got held up and can't make it."

His brother said, "Held up."

Liu Yan added, "But they're fine. You don't need to worry about them."

His oldest brother repeated, "No need to worry."

When Liu Yan said something, his brother responded. When he said nothing, his brother remained silent. It was as if Liu Yan was the oldest and his brother the youngest. After a while, his sister-in-law came over and poured him some wine, saying, "Fourth Boy, next year is a big birthday for your brother. But by convention, we are going to have the celebration this year. Let your other two brothers know."

His brother said, "Aiyah," indicating that his wife was being a busybody. But whatever his brother said, Liu Yan did not hear it. The words big birthday somehow touched his heart. And he said to his brother, "So you're sixty!"

He had forgotten all about the conversation with the elderly villagers on the road, but now, after the wine, and after realizing that his oldest brother was sixty, he felt that age was like a shadow, vague but constantly looming up in one's mind. He blurted out, "Which year were you born?"

His sister-in-law laughed and said, "Fourth Boy, you've been an official for so long that you got muddled up. You and your brother are twelve years apart – one cycle on the lunar calendar. You're of the same sign."

"So the snake?" he said.

"What snake?" his sister-in-law replied. "It's dragon."

"That's odd. I always thought I was a snake."

His sister-in-law replied, "Maybe they made a mistake when you were little." Seeing Liu Yan's consternation, she added, dismissing it in a light tone, "Never mind. A lot of people make these mistakes when they are small. My oldest sister had her age wrong by five years, and her life went on fine."

As if reading Liu Yan's mind, his brother said, "City folk are very particular about dates and ages, not like we are here in rural parts. We're a little lax about such things."

His sister-in-law was not quite happy to hear that. She said, "Whatever age Fourth Boy says he is, that's what he is, and whatever year he says he was born, that's when he was born. That does it!"

Everyone was silent after that.

Leaving his oldest brother's house, Liu Yan went with his wife and daughter to the village hotel, checking his wife and daughter into one room, while he stayed alone in another room, since he snored. In the middle of the night, he heard a dog barking, calling to mind many things from his childhood. In the end, he dreamt of his mother. He asked her urgently, "Ma, your fourth son was born in the year of the snake, right?"

His mother smiled, eyes lighting up, and said, "When my fourth was born, it was very hot. And he wasn't born when it had gotten dark. But as soon as we lit the lamp, he was born. What a coincidence!"

He said, "Ma, you're mistaken. I was born in the winter, at about seven or eight in the morning, when the sun had come up."

His mother shook her head and turned to go. He cried anxiously, "Ma! You can't go! If you go now, I'll never know when I was born."

But his mother did not even glance back.

Liu Yan cried out so loudly he woke himself up. It took him quite a while to pull himself out of the trance. He felt empty and disoriented. He looked out the window. It was light out, and there were many people moving about on the streets. Liu Yan got up, went to the door of the adjoining room, and put his ear to it. His wife and daughter were still asleep. He sent a text message to his wife, then went out by himself.

Once on the street, he asked his way to the town's police station. Getting there, he found it was already crowded with people. They surrounded a desk in a noisy crowd. He pushed his way forward, poking his head through the throng, causing the officer behind the desk to look his way and say, "Queue up!"

Eyeing him again, the officer said, "You aren't from around here?"

Liu Yan quickly replied, "No."

The officer said, "You still have to wait in line."

Liu Yan's heart sank. He noticed that everyone was looking at him. Feeling a little awkward, he went to the back of the pack. Anxious, he thought, there are so many people. Who knows how long I'll have to wait for my turn. He stood at the back, listening to the officer address each issue. After listening for a while, he felt the officer knew what was what. Although he was quite an ugly fellow, he spoke sensibly, and he seemed level-headed and mentally agile. Liu Yan settled down and waited.

Two fellows from the village were quarreling over a pig. One said his pig had run to the other's sty and refused to return. When the owner finally managed to drag the animal back home, he kept having the distinct feeling it was not his pig, but one the neighbor had secretly swapped for his own. When he went to the neighbor's house to settle it, a fight broke out, resulting in one man having his head injured and the other having his clothes ripped.

The officer listened, then said, "Where are the pigs?"

The pair answered in unison, "We've brought them along. They're in the yard."

The officer stood up from his desk, elbowing his way to the door. The crowd made a path for him and everyone – though none, aside from the two farmers, had any stake in the argument – followed the officer into the yard, where two pigs were tied to a tree. The officer inspected the creatures, smiled, and said, "Oh, they really do look alike! No wonder you two can't tell them apart."

The owner of the escaped pig pointed to one of the beasts and said, "That one's mine." But right away, he became dubious, scratching his head and said, "Or... is it that one?"

The officer said, "Even you can't tell them apart. How can you say someone furtively swapped the two?"

The fellow caught the pig, pulled up its hind leg, and said, "Look, I marked mine."

They looked and saw there was a red thread on its leg, which they had overlooked before because it was covered with dark manure. The officer said, "Is this your pig?"

The man said, "At first, it was, but then it ran away to his pen, then when he returned it, I looked and looked, and it just doesn't seem to be mine."

The officer asked the other villager, "What do you have to say about it?"

The accused man replied, "He says he marked it, and the mark is clearly on the pig's body, but he won't acknowledge it."

The other fellow said, "Who knows? The pig was in your pen for two days. Maybe you placed the mark on the other pig."

The officer said, "Can you prove it?"

The man said, "If I could prove it, I wouldn't have to come to you."

The officer replied, "But when you come to me, I need to see evidence too, and the evidence here is the mark on the pig's leg. And since this pig has the mark on its leg, that's your pig. Isn't it fine with you?"

The stubborn fellow scratched his head and said, "No, it's not."

The officer said, "Then what do you want? Do you think that pig is yours?"

Stumped by the question, the man squatted and looked the pig over once again.

The officer said, "Have you seen enough? Do you think it's yours?"

The fellow said, "I can't be sure. Anyway, I'm just not comfortable with it."

The officer asked, "Do you think it's smaller? Thinner?"

The man said, "A lot smaller and thinner."

The officer said, "Do you want a fatter pig?"

The man replied, "Of course. My pig was always fatter than his."

The officer said, "So, which of these two pigs do you think is fatter?"

The man looked at the two animals for a long time, but couldn't tell which was fatter. He said, "My eyes are now blurry…"

The officer pointed at one of the pigs and said, "There, that one's fatter."

Not yet ready to give in, the man said, "Why do I have the feeling that the other one's fatter?"

The officer said, "Bring me the scales."

At first Liu Yan thought the officer was toying with them. He never imagined that someone would actually push a weighing machine out, one rumbling along on wheels. The two creatures were tied and put on the machine, squealing for all they were worth. The pair of animals was weighed, and as if they had been working out a conspiracy, they weighed exactly the same. The officer laughed and said, "Choose whichever you want."

The fellow was still doubtful. He said, "The weight might be the same, but the meat's not. My pig ate well. His ate rubbish."

Seeing there was no difference in the two animals' weight, the other man – more liberal-minded and seemingly able to laugh off the remarks that his pig was fed on rubbish – said, "There's no need to argue. If you want to swap, let's swap." And with that, he took the rope of the pig with the marked leg and pulled it to him.

The man who had marked his pig took the lead of the other animal. When he had walked a few steps, still dubious, he said, "Is this my pig?"

The officer cursed and said, "You're a pig."

The old man said, "How can a cop curse people?"

The officer said, "You don't even know yourself, and you want to come here to dispute over a pig's identity."

The man kept quiet. He looked at the pig being led away by the other man, and felt a little reluctant to part with it. He said, "Let's swap back."

The other man, a little more easy-going now, replied, "If you want to swap back, that's fine."

The pair traded pigs. The officer laughed again and said, "What a waste of time."

When the two men and the two pigs had walked away, the next case the officer heard involved failure to care for an elderly parent. An old woman had been denied financial help from her two sons. Both sons had new houses, and their mother stayed in the old familial home. She was old and frail, and she had no source of income. The officer said, "The elder son should give you two hundred yuan, and the younger one a hundred."

Hearing this, neither son was willing to admit he was older. When the woman was consulted, she faltered, saying that her eyesight was poor and she could not be sure which was the older son.

Angry, the officer said, "You two sons, we won't differentiate between older and younger. You'll each give your mother two hundred."

Neither son was happy with this. They said, "This matter shouldn't be settled by the police. It should be settled by a judge."

The officer said, "Then take it to the court."

The two sons said, "It's no use going to court either."

The officer replied, "You know it's no use? That's good. Go away now, and each of you give your mother two hundred."

The two brothers started bickering, blaming each other in the crudest terms they could find. But they did not go so far as to fight with each other and, in the end, did as the officer had said, then left the station. Their elderly mother stumbled along behind them, crying, "Wait for me! Wait for me!"

When it was finally Liu Yan's turn, the officer was obviously very tired, but he still listened carefully to everything Liu Yan had to say. When he had finished, the officer said, "You want to confirm your age?" Then he added, "So you lost your ID card, huh?"

Liu said, "No."

The officer stared at him suspiciously. "You didn't lose your ID? Let me have a look at it."

Liu took out his ID card and handed it to the officer. With one glance, the officer smiled and said, "Look, isn't this your date of birth? Here!"

Liu said, "But when I came back to the village this time, one old fellow said I was born in the year of the rabbit, and another said the year of the dragon."

The officer said, "You mean you believe the chatter in your old hometown? You have seen for yourself just now, they can't tell their pigs – or even their sons – apart. You think they can verify what year you were born?"

Liu replied, "It's not them who wants to verify. It's me."

The officer said, "You must be joking. You don't know your own date of birth? Do you even know who you are? Comrade Liu Yan, you are a man with an identity card, and you are a man with some status."

Liu said, "But sometimes the details on an identity card are unreliable."

The officer said, "Unreliable? If you can't rely on your identity card, what can you rely on?"

Liu said, "That's why I want to get a clearer picture. In my childhood when my parents first registered my hukou, what was the date of birth under which I was registered? What year, month, and date?"

Hearing this, the officer was silent for a moment. Then he became vigilant and said, "What do you want to check your age for? Are you trying to make yourself younger? It's an old trick. I've seen plenty of people like you, trying to change their age, so they can get a promotion. Don't think you'll get anywhere with me."

Liu said, "I don't want to make myself younger, or older either. I just want to find out once and for all which year I was born. When I do find out, who knows, maybe I'll see I'm older."

The officer was surprised. "Older? Then you really are an idiot. What benefit is there in being older? To get a promotion nowadays, being young is a precious privilege. No way would anyone want to be older. In the worst cases, even being a day or two older makes a difference, not to mention a year or two."

Liu said, "I don't want to change anything. I just want to verify."

Hearing this, the officer thought for a moment, then, seemingly understanding Liu's feelings, said sympathetically, "That's true. If one doesn't even know his own date of birth, what kind of life is that?"

Liu replied, "That's right, comrade. Can I trouble you to check for me?"

The officer said, "Do you have any idea how many people and how many issues cross my desk here? Any little thing happens, and people come looking for me. I don't call this a police station. I call it a junk yard."

Though the officer was rattling on with endless complaints, at least he got up and made his way to the inner room, grumbling as he went, "I'll check. I'll check decades of records. Now, where are they...?"

Liu felt something was not quite right. No sooner had the officer gone into the room than he came back out, an embarrassed expression on his face, and said, "Sorry, those records aren't here. I must have looked in the wrong place."

Liu thought, *I knew you were going to say that.* But he did not say it. Feeling someone tug on his shirt, he turned and saw that his daughter had been standing behind him since who-knew-when. His wife was also there, standing in a corner snickering. As his daughter pulled on his shirt, Liu got distracted, and his vision blurred, so that when he looked back at the officer, he felt the man's face was vague and fuzzy. He suddenly felt deflated. He could not count on this serious, yet fuzzy officer. Having no more desire to know whether he was born in the year of the dragon, snake, or rabbit, he turned and followed his daughter out.

But the officer was not so willing to let him go. He shouted at Liu Yan from behind, "Hey! Where are you going? Wait, I'll help you search."

Liu said, "Never mind."

The officer said, "How can you not verify it? If someone doesn't know his own date of birth, what kind of life is that?"

Liu said, "I'm clear. What's on my ID is my birthdate."

The officer replied, "But sometimes there are mistakes on the ID." Seeing that Liu Yan was determined to leave, he seemed to feel some regret. Finally, he insisted, "Leave me your contact details. When I'm free, I'll definitely help you check. Then, I'll call and let you know."

The officer stared so intently at the cell phone in Liu's hand that he felt he had no choice but to leave his number.

As the family walked out, a villager pushed his way in, shouting as he squeezed past, "Qian Xingen, you bastard!"

The officer said, "Who are you calling a bastard?"

It was only then that Liu knew the officer was called Qian Xingen. The villager said, "You bastard! You fraud, I'm going to rip off your mask."

The officer replied, "Come on. If you have real guts, do it now."

Seeing that the officer wasn't bothered by his bluster, the other man softened, and speaking almost in a whisper, he said, "Do you think I don't dare?"

The officer said, "I'm waiting."

Liu and his family hurried out of the police station, so they could not hear clearly what was said after that.

All along their drive back to the city, his wife and daughter laughed about the old villagers, laughing so hard they could hardly keep from falling off their seats. Liu was not pleased. Thinking of what he had encountered at work with Mr Zhang Xiaosheng/shen/seng/sen, he said, "You shouldn't laugh at others. Some things are not just a matter of urban-rural differences."

Not knowing what had happened to him, his wife and daughter couldn't understand, so of course they did not agree with his conclusions. His wife said, "I've never seen such things in the city. I had to go to the countryside to encounter it."

When they got back home, Liu received a phone call from a teacher at his daughter's school, asking the parents to go to the school for a meeting. When Liu asked his daughter what she had done wrong at school, she replied, "I didn't do anything wrong. It could be for some commendation."

Liu asked his wife which of them should go. She said, "The teacher isn't very old, but it seems like she's going through menopause. She's always so aggressive. I'm not going."

So Liu Yan had to go. When he met the teacher, she told him that his daughter treated certain formalities like a trifling matter. She had been asked to fill up a form in duplicate and, when she wrote in her father's post at work, she wrote in two different answers. On one, she said he was Section Chief, and on the other, Department Head. The teacher said, "Mr Liu, were you promoted so quickly? Were you promoted in that brief instance between the time the first form was filled up and the second?"

In fact, Liu Yan was currently neither Section Chief nor Department Head. He was Deputy Department Head, and had been for quite some time without a sniff of a promotion in sight. It was depressing, while his daughter just made it happen – on paper.

When he went back home, he asked his daughter what she was up to. The girl replied, "Oh, I wasn't up to any sort of mischief. Just a slip of the pen."

Liu said, "You're reckless. How can you just blindly fill up the forms like that?"

Unhappy with this criticism, his daughter said, "What's the big deal? Whatever your post, you're still my father, right?" Then she added, "Why are you so upset with me? It's not like you never made a mistake, Comrade Bunny."

Enraged, Liu shot back, "Why didn't you fill in your own date of birth wrongly?"

His wife took up for their daughter, crying, "Liu Yan, what's wrong with you? Why would our daughter's birth date be wrong? She's not you. Her birth certificate is in the drawer. You want to see it?"

Liu Yan's anger rose, and he snapped in retort, "Don't be so sure! Even hospitals make mistakes."

Seeing Liu lose his temper without reason and fly into such a blind rage, his wife also became bitter. "Maybe the hospital made an even bigger mistake and confused her with another family's baby. Do you want a paternity test to make sure she's yours?"

Liu relented, "Forget it."

Several days later, a friend of Liu Yan celebrated his birthday. When Liu went to the party, he asked his friend, "Your birthday – the day, month, and year – who first told you what day it was?"

His friend thought for a while, then said, "Eh? What sort of question is that? Of course it's our parents who tell us our birthdate. You mean that isn't the case for you?"

Liu said, "My parents are deceased."

His friend hesitated, as if not sure what Liu wanted. He said, "So what? Your parents are gone. Does that mean your birthday isn't your birthday?"

Liu said, "Since your parents are still alive, you'd better check it out with them. And who says what your parents tell you is necessarily true?"

His friend replied, "They gave birth to you and raised you. Why wouldn't they know the truth?"

"Maybe the truest things are least true," Liu replied.

Not knowing what Liu was driving at with this babble, his friend ignored him and turned to greet other guests. Having overheard the conversation, another friend attending the party looked at Liu and said, "Liu Yan, it seems there's something behind your words."

Liu replied, "What about you? Do you know your birthdate? Is it your parents who told you?"

The man said, "It's written on my hukou."

Liu retorted, "Where did your hukou come from?"

The fellow rolled his eyes and turned to go away, saying nothing more to Liu.

Everyone had a lot to drink. Liu, having had his share, pointed at the birthday boy and said, "Is today really your birthday?"

Hearing Liu challenge his birthdate again, his friend was not pleased. He said, "Liu Yan, what are you getting at?"

Liu replied, "Can you be sure you were born on this date? Can you confirm with absolute certainty the year, month, and day when you were born? Are you sure you are yourself? Has it ever crossed your mind that you work so hard, and maybe it's not even your life?"

Everyone stopped upon hearing Liu's words, stunned into a long silence. The first to recover pounded the table and laughed. Pointing at the birthday boy, he said, "Aha! So, you're a bastard?"

Livid, the fellow celebrating his birthday pointed at Liu, looking like he wanted to say something, but could not, and his lips turned purple in his rage. Several people hastened to smooth things over, saying, "He's drunk! Liu Yan drank too much."

Others retorted, "Can't be. In the past, I've seen him have four or five times more without getting drunk."

Still others said, "He's wasted!"

In fact, Liu was not drunk. He just kept hearing "Happy Birthday" right and left, over and over, as if it were something real. It made him feel upset, estranged from the very words "Happy Birthday," that empty phrase. He was not even sure whose birthday it was, nor who was supposed to be celebrating it. He drank just enough to be tipsy – a subterfuge to escape the vague, phantasmagorical "birthday."

When he made his way out, his cell phone started ringing. It was an unfamiliar number. The person on the other end said, "Hello, Mr Liu, I'm the police officer." Receiving no reply from Liu, the officer went on, "Do you remember me? I'm the officer from your hometown, called Qian Xingen. Though, actually, I'm not Qian Xingen..."

Liu said, "Did you find out my birthdate?"

The officer replied, "I am calling to... well, just apologize. I'm not a police officer anymore. But it's not because I wasn't good at it. It's because I was an impostor."

Liu said, "So, even the cop was fake?"

The officer said, "Well, not exactly a fake. Qian Xingen is my cousin. When he was discharged from the military, his superior arranged for him to become a policeman. At first he agreed to it, then decided he wanted to explore some other opportunities, but it seemed a pity to lose his officer's post, so I went in and posed as him. My cousin and I look a lot alike."

Liu asked, "So you were discovered?"

The officer replied, "No, I wasn't caught, but my cousin could no longer drag out a decent living outside and wanted to come back and be a cop. He chased me out of the job, so I guess you could say I am laid off."

Liu said, "That's absurd."

The officer replied, "Not really. It's just a pity I didn't have time to look up your birthdate before it happened. Actually, I had almost got to the bottom of it. I know where the records are kept."

Liu asked, "But are those records reliable? Maybe someone made a slip from the beginning?"

The officer replied, "That's why I'm apologizing to you. I'm applying to be a cop and, if I succeed, I'll definitely look for more evidence on your behalf. I'll find irrefutable evidence to prove your date of birth."

Liu said, "So you're not Qian Xingen. What's your name then?"

The officer said, "I'm Qian Xinhai. Just one character different from my cousin's name."

Hearing this, Liu could see the officer's face clearly in front of him. Feeling a little desolate, Liu said, "Thank you, Qian Xinhai." And he hung up the phone.

WE'RE ALL IN THE SERVICE AREA

Translated by **Shelly Bryant**

Just before dawn, Gui Ping was drifting into the haze of sleep when the alarm on his cell phone started clanging nonstop. He rolled over, sat up and, as usual, first canceled the ringing sound, then turned on the phone. And as usual, almost as soon as he turned on his phone, it sounded with one incoming message after another. Gui Ping thought there were at least five or six, but after counting, he realized he had underestimated. There were seven, all sent after he had turned off the phone the previous night – one was actually sent around five that morning. It wasn't even anything urgent or important. The sender was someone who always woke up early. When he woke up, the whole family was still sleeping, and there were no signs of life on the streets outside the window either. He had probably just sent that message as a way of alleviating the loneliness of an early bird. Of these messages sent from midnight to dawn, only one required an immediate reply. None of the others were important, and Gui Ping did not have time to answer each one. He rushed to the venue, put the phone into vibrate mode, and began the meeting.

When the meeting ended, he found that matters, like the unanswered messages and phone calls, were stealthily piling up. At midday he met a client, and there was another meeting in the afternoon. At least he was able to finish his lunch in good time, so that he still had twenty minutes left after his meal. He quickly escaped into his office and lay flat on the sofa, closing his eyes to relax. But even in this brief time, his phone sounded with two more messages and three calls. Gui Ping answered the last one, feeling irritated. As soon as he saw that there were only five minutes left, click, he turned off the phone, forcing himself to close his eyes. But he felt they started to twitch involuntarily, and he simply could not close them, as if his eyelids were stuck together.

He heard his office clerk Xiao Li knock on the door. "Mr Gui, what happened to your phone? Are you in there?"

Gui Ping sat up and said dejectedly, "I'm here. I know, it's time for the meeting."

He grabbed the phone from the table and then, suddenly deciding otherwise, tossed it back on the table – perhaps a little too forcefully, for the phone swished across the table and fell to the ground with a thud. Startled, Gui Ping rushed to pick it up. Then, remembering he had turned it off, he hurried to switch it on, checked, and only relaxed when he found it undamaged. Grabbing the phone, he started to walk out of his office, but just then the phone rang. When he answered, it was an old acquaintance whose child was going to enter school, and he was hoping Gui Ping could put him in touch with some officials from the Education Bureau. Feeling the situation awkward, he knew that if he tried to get out of it, his friend would not be happy, but if he did not get out of it, he would be inviting trouble for himself. As he was thinking of what to say, Xiao Li again knocked on the door, calling "Mr Gui! Mr Gui!"

Mind alight like the flames of hell, Gui Ping told the acquaintance on the phone, "I can't talk now. I've got a meeting. Let's talk about it later."

The acquaintance said urgently, "Will it be a long meeting? What time should I call back?"

Though Gui Ping heard it clearly enough, he pretended he had not, and he hung up the phone. Still feeling frustrated, he resolutely turned off the machine once again. He tossed it on the table, flung the door open with his hands empty, and went out to the conference room.

Xiao Li followed him in confusion. "Um, Mr Gui... Where is your phone? I tried to call you just now. Why was it off? It wasn't stolen, was it?"

Gui Ping snapped, "I wish."

Xiao Li said, "Is it charging?"

"Charging my ass."

Xiao Li stuck his tongue out, not wanting to speak out of turn. Still, he couldn't help but look at Gui Ping's hand, because that hand was always carrying the phone. Seeing it suddenly empty now made Xiao Li feel strange.

There was one meeting for which the confidentiality level was high, so cell phones were not permitted. Gui Ping had left his in his office for the half-day meeting, and he felt very relaxed and worry-free. After that meeting, whenever Gui Ping felt frustrated, he would turn his cell phone off, pretending he was attending a confidential session. The dissatisfaction this had caused and the criticism it had invited were immediately evident in both his superiors and subordinates. One of his superiors said, "Gui Ping, have you been traveling abroad again? Are you always on the plane, and that's why you have to turn off your phone?"

His subordinates said, "Mr Gui, your phone is always off. If we can't reach you, do you still want us to approach you with these matters?"

Gui Ping knew he was defeated. He couldn't win the game against the phone, and he had to return to how things were.

Still nagging as he trailed behind Gui Ping, Xiao Li said, "Mr Gui, your phone's not charging. Did you forget it? Would you like me to get it for you?"

Not knowing whether he should feel amused or annoyed, Gui Ping said, "Xiao Li, sit down and we'll start the meeting."

Xiao Li finally fell silent.

In the afternoon meeting, unlike the one that morning, Gui Ping was not in the lead position, so he could duck out of the limelight and, as he usually did in such situations, take the opportunity to reply to text messages, or softly tell a new caller, "I'm in a meeting," or even, if the call was important, answer it and slip out of the conference room into the corridor to talk.

But today he had tossed his phone aside and now sat, empty-handed and relaxed, in the conference room. He felt so happy and at ease that he could not help but release a deep sigh, as if he had expelled the rancor he harbored against the phone. The feeling of freedom was like flying.

Shortly after the start of the mind-numbing meeting, Gui Ping looked at the colleagues seated around him. Some hid their phones under the conference table and yet couldn't help retrieving them, constantly looking at the screens. Others left them sitting on top of the table, but often picked them up to glance at them because, after all, the vibrating alert was not as noticeable as a ringing sound, so one might inadvertently neglect a call. When a message did come, the person's face might change, showing joy, anxiety, or calm, but none could resist exercising the thumb immediately, quickly immersing themselves in the world of the screen.

At first, Gui Ping watched them with some sympathy, seeing them controlled by their phones, unable to escape. But gradually he became antsy, the fidgeting of his hands turning into a mental unrest. Then, the calm he had felt before turned into a sort of emptiness, and the uninhibitedness morphed into anxiety, until finally, he grew emotionally volatile. Restless, he felt as if his mind were captured by the mobile phone locked in the office.

The woman sitting beside him noticed that he was uncomfortable – as if thorns were sprouting out of his body – and said, "Mr Gui, are you on your monthly flow?"

He replied, "No, I stopped flowing – I've already gone through menopause."

Everyone laughed, but it was not enough to settle Gui Ping's unease. He thought first about what day it was, then whether there might be some important phone call or message for him, or something important he needed to do, or some urgent work he had forgotten. And on top of all this, he wondered whether some extra responsibilities might have landed with him. Once he started thinking this way, more things came to mind, and he grew more anxious. His seat seemed to have sprouted a bed of nails. Finally unable to sit any longer, Gui Ping left the conference room and went to the washroom. After he finished, he stood at the door to the men's room, hesitating. In the end, he did not go back to the conference room, but to his office.

In his office, nothing was out of the ordinary, but Gui Ping had a strange feeling, as if he had been cut off from the outside world for ages. Seeing his phone on the desk, he snapped back to reality. He quickly turned it on, and a moment later a text came in. *Beep beep beep.* One message, two, three. Before he could even read them, a call came in. It was his wife, her tone urgent.

"Are you alright? You weren't in the office, and your phone was off. Are you hiding from someone?"

Unable to explain, Gui Ping simply said, "It was charging."

His wife replied, "Don't you have a spare battery?"

He answered, "I forgot to charge the other one."

His wife wondered, "The sun must have risen in the west today. Isn't your nickname 'Always On-call Gui,' and now you forgot to charge your phone?"

Gui Ping twisted his mouth in a self-deprecating smile. His wife started talking about the things she wanted him to do. In order not to prolong his wife's endless chatter, he decided to immediately agree to all her requests. Anyway, whether it's one louse or many lice, it still itches, and whether it's one debt or many debts, one still has to pay up. Gui Ping always seemed to owe other people favors. As soon as he paid one off, the next started to pop up. He was never clear of debt.

Taking his phone back to the conference room, Gui Ping started to read his messages and send replies. The woman next to him said, "Finished charging?"

He asked, "What makes you think it was charging?"

She replied, "Your phone never leaves your hand, and your hand never leaves your phone. Just now when you came to the meeting without your phone, wasn't it charging? Surely you didn't forget. Anyone else might forget to bring their phones, but you never would."

Gui Ping said, "I didn't forget. I purposely left it behind. Irritating."

She laughed again and said, "Even though you were irritated, you still ended up bringing it. You really can't get by without your phone."

Gui Ping said, "Do you really think I wouldn't dare to turn off my phone?"

She said, "Turning off your phone is no crime. There's nothing to 'dare' or 'not dare.' I just think that if you turned it off, you'd go mad."

Neither of them realized that they were speaking rather loudly until they saw one of the leaders looking at them from the rostrum. They quickly stopped talking. Gui Ping calmly read his messages, replied, and all at once rediscovered his anchor. He was no longer anxious, and he did not feel the nails poking his posterior anymore.

Before he had finished answering all the messages that needed replies, a call came in. Gui Ping looked at the number of the incoming call, but did not recognize it. Anyway, his phone was on vibrate mode, and the ringing wouldn't be heard in the conference room. He put his phone down on the thick file of materials he needed for the meeting, buffering the vibrations from his phone. The vibrations went on, but he simply ignored them. He finally felt relieved after the vibrations stopped. Then it started vibrating again, buzzing for a longer time, and more insistently. Feeling a little trapped, he finally gave in on the caller's third attempt. He had to pick up the call. He slipped down further in his seat, putting a hand over his phone, and in a muffled voice said, "I'm in a meeting."

The voice on the other end was startlingly loud. "Oh, ha ha! Gui Ping, I knew you would answer. I had already decided that if you didn't answer on the third try, I would look for someone else. But as soon as I thought that, you answered. Ha ha!"

It was a shock not only to Gui Ping's ears, but even the colleague sitting beside him could hear the voice. She said, "Aiyah, a soprano."

Even though Gui Ping said he was in a meeting, the woman did not seem to care – she went on in the same high-pitched voice, launching into the long story she had called to tell him. Gui Ping could only walk out of the conference room, clutching his phone in his palm. Only when he was in the corridor could he speak a bit louder. "I'm in a meeting. I can't always go out like that. The boss is glaring at me."

The soprano said, "What do you mean 'always go out'? I called you three times, but you only answered once. At most you only went out once."

Gui Ping thought, "People are so self-absorbed. If I answered just one call from everyone, could I survive it?" But he kept the thought to himself. He knew the soprano's temper, how she could go on a rampage and how it would end up with his defeat, so he hurriedly said, "Right. Go ahead."

The soprano finally turned to the matter she had called about. She talked and talked. Gui Ping could not help but interrupt. "I see. I'm in a meeting now. I can't leave. As soon as I can get away, I'll help you settle it."

Finally the soprano was satisfied, but she was just about to hang up when she added, "When you settle it, call my cell phone right away, OK?"

Gui Ping gave in, and got it done with, at long last. He regretted that he had not resisted. If he had not given in and answered the third call, she would have looked for someone else to take care of this. Obviously he had done fine on the first two times, so why did he give in on the third? This high-pitched woman was the type he felt quite bothersome, so he had not stored her number in his phone. And now that he had allowed her to get in touch with him, he was caught. It would be too awkward to refuse to help her with this matter. Regretting that he had not held out until the end, he grasped his phone and went back into the conference room. He ran into Xiao Li, who was sneaking out. Noticing his boss's chagrin, Xiao Li asked in concern, "Mr Gui, is everything OK?"

Gui Ping waved his phone toward Xiao Li and said, "Irritating."

Thinking he was going to throw the phone, Xiao Li quickly reached out with his hands, only to grasp at thin air. Gui Ping said, "Turning off the phone is no good. Turning on the phone is no better. It sucks."

Xiao Li observed Gui Ping's expression as he said cautiously, "Mr Gui, actually those are not the only options. There is a third possibility."

Gui Ping squinted at him and said, "On, off – what's your third option?"

Xiao Li smiled secretively, and explained that it was an option devised by people who wished to escape their loan sharks.

"What is it?" asked Gui Ping.

"Go out of the service area."

"Ha!" Gui Ping said, "How can that be – outside the service area? We aren't in a wilderness or a desert. How can we be without service?"

Xiao Li said, "Do you want to try? When your phone is on, take out the card, put back the battery, restart the phone, and then you will be outside the service area."

Gui Ping tried what Xiao Li had suggested. When he dialed his number from his office phone, he heard, "We're sorry, the number you called is not in the service area. Please try again later."

Gui Ping was thrilled. He was now free to move in and out of the service area.

Only one day after Gui Ping had resorted to this trick, the boss caught him and gave him a scolding. "I'm working myself to death. Where have you been hiding? In which mountain resort were you seeking your pleasure?"

Gui Ping hurriedly responded, "I didn't go into any mountains. I was in the office compound the whole time."

"If you were in the compound, why was your phone outside the service area?"

Gui Ping said, "But I was in the service area. I was."

The boss was furious. "Bullshit! What kind of rotten phone are you using that tells me it isn't in the service area? If you are always outside the service area, you might as well stay out of service."

Frightened, Gui Ping rectified the situation with his phone. He did not dare to leave the service area again.

Of course, Xiao Li did not escape Gui Ping's scolding. Nevertheless, he was a sort of eager beaver, indefatigable in seeking solutions for his boss. He then suggested, "Mr Gui, just forget about the trouble and store all numbers in your phone and don't leave anyone out. When you get a call, you will know whose it is and whether or not you want to answer it. The decision lies in your own hands then."

Gui Ping took this advice and purposefully applied it during the next meeting. As he sat in the conference room, he sorted through all the numbers – those he had to answer, those he could ignore, those he could afford to ignore, and those he wanted to ignore – and stored them all in his phone. As he was just about done with the task, the meeting ended. When he went out of the conference room, the phone rang. He glanced, saw it was a call he could ignore, so he simply slipped the phone into his pocket, letting it continue to ring there.

Gui Ping found this a very workable solution. He had already stored the numbers of most of the people related to him into different categories, so if he wanted to answer, he would answer, and if he wanted to ignore a call, he would ignore it. He had finally taken over control of his phone. If the caller's number was not stored in his phone, if it was an unfamiliar number, then it was definitely not someone directly associated with him and he could ignore the call.

It went on like this for a few days, and it really reduced the amount of hassle he had to deal with. Of those who usually looked for him to do them a favor, most were like the woman with the high-pitched voice. Knowing he was approachable, they came to him with all sorts of issues, big or small. Now that they couldn't reach him, they had to find other people to trouble. Even though it was a little awkward meeting them the next time, all he really had to do was to say sorry, he hadn't heard the phone, or perhaps that he had been in a meeting and it wasn't convenient to answer the call. Then it would blow over, saving him a lot of effort.

But the effort-saving days did not last long. One day, he was on his way to attend a meeting, and just as he was going into the conference room, someone tapped him on the shoulder. Startled, he looked back and saw that it was the Administrative Deputy Minister of the Organization Department of the CPC. With a smile on his face, he said, "Mr Gui, you've been busy, huh?"

Gui Ping's heart skipped a beat at first, then he started to wonder in his mind. His relationship with the deputy minister was not close to the point of bantering with each other. He quickly tried to turn the table on the deputy minister, and tested the waters, "Not too bad. I'm busy, but not nearly as busy as you."

The deputy minister smiled and said, "Whether you're busy or just messing around, whatever the case, all I know is you're busy. Why else would you not answer my phone calls?"

This gave Gui Ping a huge fright, making his heart pound. He stuttered a few times, then said, "Mr – Mr Minister, you called me?"

"When I called your office, you weren't there. When I called your cell phone, you didn't answer. Then I knew you were a difficult man to reach."

Gui Ping, really panicking now, resorted to the truth. "Mr Minister, I didn't know it was you calling."

The deputy minister smiled. "You mean you didn't store my number in your phone? I must not be very important to you then." Knowing Gui Ping was nervous, the deputy minister slapped him on the shoulder, making him relax a little. "Don't worry, anyway it is not about your promotion. If it were, I am not supposed to call you in person."

Embarrassed, Gui Ping laughed. The deputy minister continued, "So don't worry, you didn't miss anything. I just wanted to ask you to take care of someone. He was assigned to your Reform Commission. I just wanted to ask you to keep an eye on him, make him feel at home. Just a joke. Don't you office directors all like to be called by fancy titles like the palace chamberlain? Well, this young fellow had just entered your unit, and if he had the palace chamberlain's attention, it would have made a great difference, wouldn't it?"

Anxious, Gui Ping asked, "Who is it? Which department is he with?"

The deputy minister said, "I don't need you to look after him now. He's not in your unit anymore. He was transferred a couple of days ago. Don't worry, it's nothing to do with you. Nowadays, it's normal for young guys to job-hop. If he didn't, that'd be rare. So we can just leave them alone."

As they were talking, the deputy minister walked into the conference room with Gui Ping, his manner almost affectionate. Many people in the conference room noticed it and one commented later, "I didn't know you were so close to the deputy minister."

Gui Ping was very upset. The opportunity had been right on his doorstep, and he had slammed the door in its face. But how could he have known the deputy minister would call his line directly? Looking at it now, taking such a strict approach to governing the strange numbers on his phone had been a mistake. A big mistake. Huge. Admitting a mistake meant it was time for change. Gui Ping found the directory of the leading cadres, all the leaders – anyone who was on the directory – and entered the numbers into his phone. Fortunately his current phone's memory was large. Storing that many numbers would not make it explode.

Now Gui Ping could finally relax. He could avoid unnecessary troubles, but also would not miss out on an opportunity when it came his way. But after a long, long time, not a single high official called his phone. Still, he was not worried, and he did not feel the effort was wasted. He was prepared. Forewarned was forearmed.

A few days later, Gui Ping's classmates from university held a gathering for all those who still lived in the city. Over the years, some had left, some had come back, and some had come back and left again. Now, what was left could just fill up one table. On that day, everyone seemed to be in good mood, and all came.

As soon as they sat down, they all took their cell phones out from a bag or pocket, setting them on the table where they were sure to always be in sight amid the dishes and wine glasses there. Gui Ping did not take his out, leaving it in his back pocket, set on vibrate as well as ring mode. If the gathering was lively and everyone was speaking loudly and he missed the ringing, he would still feel the vibration on his rear. It was almost foolproof. There were also a couple of the more reserved female classmates who did not take their phones out and place them on the table, but they held their bags close and unzipped, not obstructing the sound of the phones' ringing. In this way they could drink and reminisce without a worry.

The conversation was very lively and engaging, with many of the classmates' old romances – whether open or secret – being the topic of discussion. There were some romances that seemed really heartbreaking at the time, so painful those involved felt like dying. Discussing these romances, after so many years had passed, had become a sort of enjoyment. Whether they had been directly involved in the tale or merely spectators, they all enjoyed the light touch of sadness and happiness brought on by time.

When they had finished talking about old times, they started to discuss the present. Now this one was having an affair, that one had a way with women, who was whose mistress, who was doing what with whom, and so on. Then one classmate pointed at another and said, "I saw you the other day shopping with some woman. It wasn't your wife, so I didn't dare call you."

Everyone coaxed him, urging him to tell all. He happened to be an honest but untactful guy, and he kept swearing and denying anxiously, but no one believed him. Exasperated, he looked here and there, as if looking for something to prove his innocence. Then they saw him take out his phone and fling it on the table. "Take out your phones," he said.

Most people's phones were already on the table. Several pushed theirs forward, while others pulled theirs back, but no one knew what he wanted to do. Then he said, "If there is anything going on, the phone will be full of secrets. Who dares? Let's all exchange phones and see each other's contents. If you have secrets, you won't dare. But I dare!"

As soon as he finished saying this, a couple of the friends turned pale and quickly reached for their phones. One said, "A phone is private. How can we just swap and look at each other's phones? What are you, a voyeur?"

And of course there were others who did not panic, but were quite open. Some were even excited by the idea, saying, "Look. Go ahead. Let's lay everything bare here on the table."

Gui Ping didn't care either way, but he did feel that this naive classmate was going a little overboard. He said, "Who would be silly enough to keep that kind of message? You think anyone would want to bring it home for a spouse to read?"

The classmate obstinately rebutted, saying, "If you really feel that way about someone, you can't bear to delete the messages."

Everyone laughed, saying he obviously had some experience in this area, since he knew how it really felt. It went on for a while until the classmate could not withstand their assault and so, red-faced and angry, he shoved his phone into another classmate's hand and said, "Come on. Take a look."

And so the group was divided into two camps, those willing to share the secrets of their phones and those who refused to participate in the game, keeping their phones firmly clutched in their hands, afraid someone might snatch them. Another group, including Gui Ping, were either not afraid at all, or at least pretended they didn't care, hoping to save their face. They all put their phones on the table, and the one who had suggested the game mixed them up with his eyes closed. Then everyone closed his or her eyes and picked one. Gui Ping got hold of a female classmate's phone. Just as he started to inspect it, he sneaked a look at her, noticing how embarrassed she looked. Something inside him stirred, and he said, "Forget it. I don't want to look at a woman's phone."

He handed the phone back to her and she put it away. However, she would not rest her sharp tongue. She said, "Why don't you look? It's your own loss if you don't."

He didn't bother about her, but his own luck was not so good. His phone had been taken by one of the nosiest guys in the group.

The first thing the fellow did was to look through the messages. Disappointed, he said, "Hm. You're well prepared."

Gui Ping said, "Of course. If not, why would I take it out and let you look?"

But the fellow would not give up so easily. He inspected the phone book to see if he could find any suspicious characters there.

A look of shock came over him. The fellow's face reddened and he blurted out, "Gui Ping, you're so influential. You even have the higher-ups' cell numbers." He went through the names stored in Gui Ping's phone, reading them out one by one. "These are all the big wigs and VIPs."

The stunned group of classmates all turned to stare at Gui Ping, saying things like, "Wow, you are sly. Such an impressive background, and you never told us."

One also said, "It's called keeping a low profile, you know? A low profile is the thing these days."

Unable to offer a good explanation, Gui Ping could only laugh it off.

He had not imagined how long the echoes of this laughter would follow him. The next day, a former classmate sought him out at his office, a weighty gift in hand, asking Gui Ping to help contact the Deputy Mayor in charge of the cultural industry. The classmate was planning the city's biggest, highest standard video game arcade. The Department of Culture had given the green light, but the documents were not signed by the Deputy Mayor, and they could not proceed without his signature. He had tried to get in touch with the Deputy Mayor several times, but always came back empty-handed. Now it all depended on Gui Ping's power.

Knowing that this sort of apparition came through the door opened by his phone, Gui Ping had to say frankly, "Actually, I don't know the deputy mayor."

His classmate said, "Impossible. You have his number in your phone. How can you not know him?"

Gui Ping confessed the truth of what had happened, beginning to end. Hearing it, his classmate said, "Ha! Gui Ping, since you became an official, you've become more twisted. I'm surprised you don't have state leaders' numbers stored in your phone."

Gui Ping joked, "If I knew their numbers, I would have stored them too."

His classmate was angry. He said, "Tell me in good conscience, all these years you've been working for the government and I've been struggling in the private sector, have I ever come to you with any kind of trouble? Just this once. One time I come to you and you refuse me. Is that fair?"

Gui Ping knew that no matter what he said, his classmate would not believe him, but there was also no way he could approach the Deputy Mayor. He could only put on a cold expression and say, "Anyway, you can think what you like, it doesn't matter. There's nothing I can do to help in this matter."

Angry, his classmate left, but did not take the gift with him. Gui Ping felt like shouting for him to come back, but he thought that would be going too far, so he did not call after his friend.

The pile of gifts was left sitting there. Whenever Gui Ping saw them, he felt awful. He moved them into a corner of the room, but his eyes kept roaming there involuntarily. He cleared a space in the cupboard, put them inside, and closed the cupboard door, feeling better once he was rid of the sight of them. All along, he had enjoyed a harmonious rapport with his classmates, but now that perfect feeling was ruined by the mistake he had made, storing these numbers in his phone. He went back and forth in his mind, trying to decide if it was really wise to input the numbers of all those officials, both those he knew and those he didn't. He picked up his phone, ready to delete the unnecessary numbers, but could not decide which to keep and which to discard. It didn't feel right to delete them all, so in the end he did nothing.

At first he worried that he had offended his classmate, but then he hardened his heart. *If he's offended, he's offended. I'll make up for it when I get the chance.*

But he did not realize that the offense would not be so easily resolved. After a couple of days, the classmate came again. Changing his tactic, he came into the office and sat on the sofa. He said, "I'm not leaving until you promise to help me."

Gui Ping said, "I have work to do. It's not convenient for you to just sit there."

His classmate said, "It's convenient for me."

"But not for me," Gui Ping replied.

"What's not convenient? Just pretend that you've set something on the couch, it should be fine. Do your work. It's not like you're in the secret service. If I overhear you working, I'm not going to announce it to anyone. And even if I do, no one is interested."

And with that he attached himself to Gui Ping's office with a death grip.

Even so, Gui Ping could not make this phone call, because he really had no contact with this deputy mayor at all, no connections. His line of work was not under the supervision of this mayor. Even if they had been together in any meeting, the deputy mayor was sitting at the rostrum, and Gui Ping could only catch a glimpse of him from a distance. There were always many officials at the rostrum, and this deputy mayor would have just been one figure in the crowd. Aside from that, he might have glimpsed the deputy mayor on the local news on TV. They only shared an on-rostrum-off-rostrum – onscreen-offscreen sort of relationship. How would it look for him to approach this deputy mayor with some business not his own, and especially such sensitive business as planning a giant video game arcade?

So his classmate sat on the sofa. When people came in to report or discuss work matters, he just looked away, showing he was not interested in Gui Ping's work. Even if Gui Ping felt it was nothing, others found it strange and felt stifled, too uncomfortable to say directly what they had come to say. What should have been simple matters thus became complicated. After a half-day of it, Gui Ping was both physically and mentally exhausted. It was too much. He said to his classmate, "You stay here. I'm going to the washroom."

The classmate said, "You can't escape."

Gui Ping just wanted to slip outside, regain his composure, and think of countermeasures, but he could not just stand there in the corridor while he thought, so he went to the washroom. After spending quite some time there, he still had no clue what to do, and he couldn't simply stay in the toilet, so he made his way back to his office again. But who would have imagined that the classmate would gleefully greet him at the door. Gui Ping said, "What are you smiling about?"

His classmate said, "Everything is fine. I used your phone to call the deputy mayor, and he said to wait for his call."

Gui Ping started. "You – you – what have you done?"

"I didn't do anything wrong. It all went just fine!"

"What did you say to the deputy mayor?"

"Of course I didn't say it was me. I said it was you."

For a moment, Gui Ping didn't understand. "What do you mean it was me?"

I said, "Deputy Mayor, this is Gui Ping from the Reform Commission."

Anxiety flooded over Gui Ping. "He doesn't even know me. What did he say?"

"Oh, Come on! He knows you very well. He said very warmly, 'Oh yeah, Gui Ping!'

Then I said, 'I have a relative who needs to see you about an important document.'"

Gui Ping said, "How could you talk such nonsense? You, my relative?"

"Classmate, relative – it's all the same. Why the fuss? If I were your relative, would that be a loss of face?"

Gui Ping felt he was being choked, and he couldn't speak for a moment. Enraptured, his classmate continued, "The deputy mayor said he would get his secretary to arrange a time and inform me as soon as he could. Oh! Not me, but you."

He had hardly finished when Gui Ping's phone rang again, and it really was the deputy mayor's secretary, asking, "Is that Director Gui with the Reform Commission? The deputy mayor has time tomorrow afternoon at four, but at most he only has half an hour. He has a reception at five."

Gui Ping was astounded, but he knew there was no way out. He could never say that the person who had just called was not him, but that someone had used his phone without his knowledge.

Fearing Gui Ping might give the game away, his classmate winked at him desperately. Gui Ping glared at him, but he really was helpless in the whole affair, so he promised the deputy mayor's secretary that he would be at the office the next day at four for a half-hour meeting.

When he hung up, his classmate was overjoyed. Gui Ping, on the other hand, was puzzled, and kept saying, "How could that be?"

His classmate wasn't angry anymore. He said, "Anyway, as things stand, you'll have to come with me tomorrow. Don't worry. I won't come empty-handed."

Angry, Gui Ping said, "I've never encountered a person like you."

The classmate, on the other hand, left happily.

When his classmate had gone, Gui Ping called Xiao Li in and asked, "Xiao Li, do I know this Deputy Mayor?"

Confused, Xiao Li replied, "Mr Gui, what do you mean?"

Gui Ping said, "I don't remember having any dealings with him, but he hasn't been the deputy mayor for very long, has he?"

Xiao Li said, "Since the beginning of the year during the session of National People's Congress, so not more than two or three months."

Gui Ping said, "Well, he's never been in charge of our division. At most, he's been on the rostrum once or twice when I was seated below. He's way beyond my reach I believe."

Xiao Li said, "That's true. I've also seen those leaders high on the rostrum from way below where I was sitting. Which leader would notice me sitting there below the rostrum?"

Noticing Gui Ping's frown, Xiao Li wanted to take the initiative to play the role of problem-solver. He said, "Mr Gui, maybe sometime before he was the deputy mayor, you two came into contact. Maybe it was a long time ago, so you forgot, but the deputy mayor has an exceptional memory, so he didn't forget."

Gui Ping said, "Before he was the deputy mayor, where was he working?"

Xiao Li said, "Let me think." After a moment, it came to him. "He was in the Fisheries Bureau. He was an expert, and also a member of one of the democratic parties. When the government changed, they saw a need for this kind of person, so they selected him. Later I heard that he joked about it. 'I never dreamed I would become a deputy mayor.'"

Gui Ping said, "The Fisheries Bureau? Then all the more I don't know him. I've never had any dealings with the Fisheries Bureau."

Xiao Li thought for a moment, and then said, "Or else, there is another possibility. Perhaps the deputy mayor's memory isn't exceptionally good, but exceptionally bad. Maybe he's confused and has you mixed up with someone else. Maybe he thinks you're that person."

Gui Ping said, "Surely he couldn't be that confused."

Xiao Li replied, "Or maybe the deputy mayor is really busy and he assumed that anyone who approached him or anyone who called his cell phone must at least be an acquaintance. Think about it, a stranger surely wouldn't just call a deputy mayor's cell phone."

But no matter how Xiao Li analyzed it, nothing seemed to clear it up for Gui Ping. After Xiao Li left, Gui Ping took out his phone and looked at it. Looking at the number of the deputy mayor's secretary who had just called, he thought, *This is a landline, probably the secretary's office phone.* Then it suddenly struck him that he did not even know the surname of this deputy mayor's secretary. He only knew that the secretary had not been in this post very long. Gui Ping frantically asked around and learned the secretary's surname, then his fingers flew over the phone and he called the secretary again.

The call was answered promptly. The voice on the other end said, "May I ask who's calling?"

Gui Ping said, "This is Gui Ping, from the Reform Commission. Just now – just now–"

The secretary had a good memory. He immediately said, "Director Gui, your meeting with the mayor has already been arranged for tomorrow afternoon at four. Is there anything else?"

Gui Ping faltered for a moment, not quite sure what to say. He paused, then said, "I wanted to ask, are you free tonight–?"

Out of habit, the secretary immediately reacted strongly. "Director Gui, there's no need."

Gui Ping wanted to explain, but the secretary seemed to think Gui Ping wanted to treat him to dinner and present him with gifts, so he refused, saying, "Director Gui, you don't need to bother. I know you are one of the deputy mayor's close associates, and whatever the deputy mayor asks us to do, we'll give it our best effort."

Testing the waters, Gui Ping asked, "What makes you think I'm one of the deputy mayor's close associates?"

The secretary laughed and said, "The mayor usually doesn't answer his cell phone. He gave it to me to manage. Most of the calls are screened by me before I ask the mayor for his decision. But when you called today, he answered himself. Doesn't that say it all?"

Speechless, Gui Ping could only give up.

When his work day ended and Gui Ping went home, his mind was a mess. His wife noticed and asked, "What happened?"

Gui Ping could not even say what all had happened, but could only sigh heavily several times. Just as his wife was growing suspicious, his phone rang. Gui Ping looked and saw that it was his classmate calling. He was already driven mad by this classmate, so why would he answer the call? He let the phone ring. The ringing continued insistently. His wife said, "Why don't you answer? Are you afraid to take the call with me sitting here?"

Gui Ping snapped, "I just don't want to answer."

Overwhelmed by her suspicions, his wife reached out, grabbed his phone, and yelled. "Who is that? Why are you so clingy?"

When she heard a male's voice on the other end, she lost interest. She shoved the phone into Gui Ping's hand and walked away bored. Gui Ping held the phone. Even though he was overwhelmed with reluctance, he could hear the, "Hello? Hello? Hello?" on the other end of the line.

"Yeah?" he said sharply. "What are you hollering at?"

He was about to throw in a few more harsh words, but his classmate started, "Gui Ping, I don't need to bother you tomorrow after all."

Gui Ping was surprised, then overjoyed, but before he could say anything, his classmate continued, "I won't trouble you tomorrow, but it doesn't mean I won't bother you forever." Then he added, "I just got word from the Cultural Affairs Department that a file from high-level administration has arrived, saying that the planning of all video game arcades or shops has been suspended. The project is to be overseen at the provincial level now and it is no longer within the mayor's capacity."

Gui Ping hesitated for a long time, and then started laughing. "You're joking, right? What is going on? The guy at the deputy mayor's office has already made the appointment, and now you want me to inform the mayor that we don't need to see him?"

The classmate laughed, "Then you just go see him about another matter."

Gui Ping said furiously, "Don't come asking me for help again."

The classmate was still laughing. "No way," he said. "I'll still have to rely on you later."

Gui Ping said, "You just said all your approvals will come from the provincial level. I don't know anyone at the provincial level."

His classmate said, "Come on. If you know so many city leaders, your contacts must be very far-reaching. I'm sure you can get in contact with a few provincial leaders. But, it's not time yet. Things are not very clear. I'll know something soon, though, and if I need help with the provincial leaders, I'll have to get you to run to the provincial office with me when the time comes."

So angry he could spit blood, Gui Ping said, "I'm changing my cell phone number."

His classmate laughed, "Do you think people won't recognize you anymore just because you put on a disguise?"

The next day, Gui Ping had to think hard to find an excuse to go to the deputy mayor's office. When he saw the stately deputy mayor, he started to panic, as if the fellow could see right through him. Suddenly he was unable to articulate the excuse he had made up for this meeting. Just as he was wondering how he could extricate himself from the mess, the deputy mayor smiled and said, "You're Gui Ping, from the Reform Commission? Actually, I don't remember meeting you before."

Gui Ping, terrified, said, "Then why did you agree to see me?"

"Ah, that's a long story," the deputy mayor said, looking at his watch. "Anyway, since we've got half an hour to talk, I'll tell you about it. I'm sure everyone knows that my cell phone is always managed by my secretary, so he always has my phone in hand. I never look at or listen to it. I know nothing at all about it. All the calls are answered by him, and he arranges all my appointments. I am at his mercy, and he leads me around by the nose. I have no freedom, because it's always been like that in bureaucracy. It was much the same with the former deputy mayor as with the one before him. I am in no position to change it." He paused for a moment, then went on, "And you also know, I had my own specialty before and was suddenly put in this post. I have not really adapted to it yet, so I've just been bearing with it here at first. Right up until yesterday afternoon, when I finally couldn't stand it anymore, and I was determined to take back my right to use my own cell phone, so I just asked my secretary to return it to me. Just as he handed me the phone, the first call came in, and it was you. My secretary was standing there watching me. I wanted him to know that I was perfectly capable of managing my work without him, so I instructed him to arrange a time for our meeting. See, that's what happened."

Gui Ping froze for quite a while, thinking the deputy mayor was joking. But then from the look on the man's face, that did not seem to be the case. He faltered, uncertain what to say. The good news was that the deputy mayor did not want to hear anyway. He sighed and waved Gui Ping off. "Never mind. From now on, this sort of thing won't happen. You won't be able to reach me on my cell phone. I returned it to my secretary. I threw in the towel, since I can't win anyway. Yesterday, I spent the whole afternoon from the time you called onward answering twenty-three phone calls. All were asking for help from the mayor. Damn, I give up." He paused, and then added one final thought, "Alas, now I know it's not easy being a secretary, let alone an office director."

Gui Ping said, "That's true. It's aggravating."

The deputy mayor looked at him, then said, "Right. I still haven't asked, Director Gui, since I've never met you, how did you come to call my cell phone?"

Gui Ping also laid the matter out before him honestly. The deputy mayor listened, then laughed for a moment. Gui Ping could not tell whether or not there was any amusement in the laughter.

After experiencing this false alarm, Gui Ping immediately changed his number. He only informed a handful of friends, family, and close work associates, not saying anything about it to the rest. As a result, he created for himself, and others, a lot of hassle and invited a lot of criticism. But no matter what happened, Gui Ping just gritted his teeth and bore with it, determined to put his old cell phone troubles behind him. He wanted to say farewell to the bygone days, to live for himself, to take himself firmly in hand and not be controlled by the phone.

But now that his phone lay quietly on his desk, Gui Ping still had no peace of mind, feeling as uncomfortable as if hundreds of tiny worries were clawing at his heart. The phone did not disturb him, but he went and disturbed the phone. After a while, he picked it up and looked at it, wondering if he had missed something. But there was nothing. Gui Ping began to suspect that the problem was with the ring tone. So he switched it to vibrate mode. The phone would not vibrate. He picked it up and dialed the office number. The call went through. Then he picked up the office phone and dialed his mobile number. It went through too. He waited, but still nothing came from the phone. He messaged his wife. "You OK?" The message went out normally, and his wife quickly replied, "What do you mean?" He received that without any problem either.

His wife's reply seemed to contain some smell of gunpowder. Sure enough, no sooner had he received her message than she called, asking, "What are you up to?"

Gui Ping replied, "It's strange. No one has called or texted all day."

"You're the strange one. When you get lots of calls, you always complain. Today when you have a rare moment of rest, it's like you have ants in your pants."

After his wife hung up, Gui Ping was certain that there was no problem with his phone, but he still couldn't sit still. He called a colleague and said, "Did you call my cell phone this morning?"

"No," the colleague replied.

He called another friend and asked, "Did you text me this morning?"

"No," his friend replied.

Gui Ping kept watch over this new number, which was as quiet as death, and he could not help missing his old number. Using his new number, he dialed the old line. He heard the message, "We're sorry, the number you are dialing has been disconnected."

He started to panic.

He called Xiao Li to come in and took it out on him, "You disconnected my old line?"

Xiao Li replied, "Eh, Mr Gui, didn't you ask me to change your number?"

Gui Ping said, "I told you to change my number, but I didn't say I don't want the old one anymore. I've had that number for many years. There's sentimental value. Now you've just tossed it away?"

Xiao Li said, "Mr Gui, don't worry. It hasn't been tossed aside. I suspended the number, but still held it for you. It just costs five yuan a month, and the number is still yours. You can restore it whenever you want."

Gui Ping was distracted for a moment, and then said, "What made you decide to hold the number?"

Xiao Li said, "Mr Gui, I had a sixth sense. I just thought you might want it back."

Gui Ping wanted to ask, *What made you think I'd want it restored?* But before the words reached his lips, he decided not to ask. Even such a lightweight as Xiao Li could see him through and this was simply too much for him, so he hardened himself and said, "I don't want it. Go now and get rid of the number for good."

Xiao Li said, "OK. Sure. I'll save that five yuan for you."

By that afternoon though, the situation had changed dramatically. The calls coming into his phone had increased greatly, as had the incoming messages. There were many from people whom Gui Ping was sure he had not informed of his new mobile phone. Still, they kept calling. Gui Ping said, "Ah, this is strange. How did you know my number?"

The caller said, "Who do you think you are? Is it a big deal to know your number?"

There were also some who retorted, "You're the one acting strange. Why can't I know your number?"

Then there were some who were overly sensitive, "So what? Do you regret it? You don't want to be in contact with me anymore?"

And so Gui Ping resumed his old life, the cell phone busy from morning until night. This was normal life for Gui Ping. He had adapted to it early on. He resumed complaining about how irritating the cell phone was, but he also continued to be attached to it. He only found it strange how so many people came to know his new number.

It was many days later that he finally learned what had happened. After his talk with Xiao Li, the latter had secretly replaced his new phone memory card with the old.

THE
HALLUCINATED
COURIER

Translated by **Edward Allen**

One day I made a courier delivery to someone's home. The receiver was a young girl – just the type who is fiercely loyal about shopping online. She came out of her room, took her delivery, and asked me for a pen to sign her receipt. So as to remind her, I said, "Open up and check the goods first."

This was on no account due to my own sense of responsibility. It's a company regulation. The company stipulates that we must first have the recipient open the package up before signing for receipt. Otherwise, any later consequences will invariably befall us couriers. Since there was no wish on my part to put up with so many consequences, I was firm in having her open her parcel before she signed. The young girl seemed a bit impatient, as if she didn't really care that much for the goods I was delivering. She hummed and hawed and said, "Aiyoh, let's just not open it. I'm busy."

"That won't work." I said, "It can't be signed for if it's not been opened, unless..."

"Unless what?" she asked, hurriedly.

"Unless you make it clear in writing on the receipt."

She asked what she should write, and I said, "You write that the receiver of this parcel voluntarily leaves the parcel unopened and uninspected, that this has no connection whatsoever with the person making the delivery, that you are responsible for all consequences, and so on. Then you sign your name."

This got her worked up again. "Aiyoh!" She said, once more, "What a bore! You want me to write that much? Oh, whatever! Whatever! I'll just open it up and have a look."

But the parcel was wrapped up very tight, and she frowned and thought once more about humming and hawing through. Fortunately, I always carried around a small knife, which cut through the cellotape gripped around the package. This knife of mine was used specially to deal with those people who took delivery of a package but were afraid of any bother. Those people would take the lack of a tool to open their package as an excuse to forcibly sign the receipt, to hum and haw away and stumble through the matter. I did not permit such practices.

Of course, not all recipients are like this girl. The habits of some people turned out to be the complete opposite. It put me at my wit's end to see the levels they went to check the authenticity of goods I handed over. There was, for example, a woman who liked to buy clothes from the internet. Every time she got her hands on the clothes, she would inspect them over and over, looking up and down, front and back, inside and out, even poking around the seams to have a good look. I watched from the side, chuckling to myself – maybe she thought that I was the one who'd sown the item together? But even if she found a problem with the seams, what could she have me do about it? There was another woman who would buy clothes with some regularity. On one occasion, she got a whiff of rubber after she'd opened her package for inspection. She insisted that this was some fake, low-grade product and demanded on the spot that it be sent back. She then said that wearing such clothes could give you cancer. It scared the hell out of me. Still, whether goods were real and the price was right, or whether they were just shabby fakes, neither had anything to do with me. All she was doing was making my life difficult, and I patiently went through with her the regulation whereby, when goods are inspected, only damaged products or those not matching the agreed-upon size and colors could be returned, explaining that there was no rule stating that odd-smelling clothes could be rejected on the spot. Finally, after grinding away for what seemed like half a day, she began to talk sense. She accepted the possibly terrifying clothes, though resolving to make a call later to our customer-service line and demand the product be returned. I never heard what came of this afterward, and, anyway, it didn't concern me. Then there was this really odd recipient who simply had to ask me for my name. I said that the company didn't stipulate that we give our names out and that I could just not tell her. However, when she persisted, I just told her, kidding myself that she might be thinking of hooking me up with a marriage partner. I wasn't expecting that the next time I went she would ask me for my name again.

"I told you last time." I said.

"My memory's bad," she replied. "I've forgotten."

So I told her again.

This happened over and over, each time I visited. In the end I became quite suspicious about it all. I explained to her that a courier's name was hardly that important.

"How could it not be important?" she asked. "I even ask the names of the men who carry up the water."

I supposed she was defending herself against any unforeseen problems, fearing that when someday something should go wrong, she could not find the wrongdoer. In actual fact, she was ignorant of a rule in all delivery companies – one courier per district. It was all very clear, and she'd just have to state her address and the company would know who had delivered her goods. This didn't hold for those companies that didn't play by the rules – they wouldn't notify the seller unless they know the courier's name. But in such a case, what was the difference even if you knew the name of the boss – it was useless just the same.

Truly, when the forest grows large, there are all kinds of birds. One must to be careful in their dealings with each different bird – no one was forced to be a courier anyway. Mistakes were frequent in deliveries nowadays, but no matter who was wrong or right, the bird always shit on a person's head. The only choice anyone had was to act like they were treading on thin ice, so as to protect their head from the bullying birds.

But no more of birds – back to the matter at hand. At length, the woman opened her parcel and took out the goods. I was not in the mood to care much for what she had – even a magician's Invisibility Box would have had nothing to do with me – but she just had to take the item and dangle it in front of my face.

"Hey! You see that?"

I made a pretense of eyeing up the goods – a pair of leggings... magenta, even. In my mind I started to hold her in very low regard. Don't think that I didn't know full well that those leggings go for nothing more pricey than a few dozen yuan online! The cheapest go for just ten! She didn't feel any embarrassment on account of these cheap, cheerful leggings. "Okay, well, I've checked, so I can sign the receipt, now?" she said, her flourishing complete.

Of course she could sign. It wasn't as if I was intentionally trying to catch her out here. Everything was fine as long as she went by the regulations, so I politely asked her to sign her name on the receipt. I tore off the top-sheet, and I was good to go. She had already returned to her room, but as I was turning away, I heard her give out a piercing scream from inside. Thinking some mistake had been made, I jerked back my head and had a look in her direction, only to see her doubled up with laughter, arching her back as she howled –

"AI – YOH – YOH! AI – YOH – YOH!"

Now, I had no idea what she was aiyoh–ing about with such vim, but since she was not trying to make any trouble for me, I hastened my escape. Seeing me make off, she forced herself to straighten her back.

"AI – YOH!" she blurted at me. "I've already bought a pair that's exactly the same! Ai – yoh! How could I have just totally forgotten about it? I completely forgot. But seeing this pair, I'm reminded that I bought one just a few days ago."

But this had nothing to do with me, so there was no reason for me to stay. Off she went again, "I can't be going gaga! I'm only twenty-five!"

Even so, this had nothing to do with me, and I recommenced my escape. At long last I was able to run off.

There was some novelty value when I started out in this trade, but this feeling had all gone with the passing of time. Everything was in the same mould. It was like the recipients. I'd say seventy to eighty percent of them were just like that little bitch with the leggings. They got some cash in their hands – not a lot, mind you – and they splurged it all online on some worthless or basically useless stuff. I really could not make sense of these women, with their itchy hands, as if no day could pass without them getting on a computer-mouse and clicking here, clicking there, and clicking again over there. Naturally, it was because of this daily clicking, additional clicking, and further clicking that the delivery companies had sprouted like bamboo shoots after the spring rain, constantly increasing in numbers and power. I've even heard that there are over a thousand delivery companies now. A colleague of mine commented, "Over one thousand? Whose total is that? Does it cover those shady companies which can't even be found on the records?"

This colleague had a more fertile mind than I. There were over a thousand according to the statistics, but according to his way of thinking, there was no way of knowing just how many companies there were. No wonder the competition was so intense.

Naturally, again, amongst the countless recipients, it was not certain that these women received things that they bought with their own money. There were instances of other people sending things as gifts or buying the item for them. "Oh! My boyfriend!" "Mom and Dad!" Or someone-else. But this was a very small percentage.

As a matter of fact, I shouldn't moan about these women, much less look down on them, since with these girls came the business of delivery companies and our rice bowl for the day. In fact, there were quite a number of decent girls among them. They would be pretty excellent if their hands didn't get so itchy. I would have been a happy man if I could find any one of them to be my wife.

There was one time I made a delivery to a home. The girl opened the door and, courteously, pressed me to come inside. I knew my place, so I wouldn't go in. Yet she became extremely enthusiastic, even moving over and pulling me inside.

"Come in! Come in! There's no problem!" she said.

Even so I only stood in the entrance to her home. In this way I could take a casual glance inside. Wow! She'd piled up half her room with courier deliveries, most of them unopened, bundled up dead-tight! I couldn't tell which company had delivered these – how could they make a delivery without having the parcels opened up first? Still, that had nothing to do with me, and I was alright as long as I got my work done. What was the use in occupying oneself with what other delivery companies were up to? Each company had its rules and regulations. I did think, however, that it would be best not to marry this kind of woman. She was plainly making purchasing a part of her little game. How could a courier such as I have the money to play mom and dad with her?

Would you call this a sense of inferiority, or was it truly a sense of inferiority? Would you call this one-sided wishful thinking, or was it truly one-sided wishful thinking?

That was a kaleidoscopic picture of those who receive deliveries. As for the senders of these items, I didn't see them, but I did know that they came in all shapes and sizes. I just couldn't be bothered to say more, with them out of sight.

It would have been best if I had taken a little more concern for myself. Sometimes, arriving at a residential district, I had the feeling that I was dreaming. Why was I dreaming? Because I was so overly familiar with these districts, and they were all so alike that although I went into different districts every day, they appeared all the same and indistinguishable from each other. I not only saw them in my dreams, but actually took them as a dreamland during my waking life.

In fact, you didn't have to go into these districts yourself – you just closed your eyes and thought about it. Could it be any other way? How could those numerous newly built-up districts not come in more or less the same style? Buildings standing like matchboxes in their place, one block glued to the next, with some stuck together a bit more tightly, and some with a bit more space in between – and that was the sole difference between one district and another. The former we called a common district, and the latter we referred to as a posh district. As for the slight discrepancies in shape and color that existed between these buildings, this was far from being the key to the point. They were mere superficialities. We were all grown-ups, so such superficialities as these were not going to blinker us.

Then you scouted out a certain building, headed to a certain room, took the elevator for the high-rises or climbed the stairs for the lower ones. You knocked on the door or rang the bell, and someone asked, "Who is it?"

"Delivery!" you said.

Then the door opened, you took a peek inside. Never mind the similarities between one building and another. There was never much difference even in the interior decoration.

If you were to go through every single day in a space and a time much like this, perhaps you, also, would find it hard to make sense between the time you were dreaming and the time you were awakened from your dreams.

Alright, alright. No more of dreams. Right then I had already made my way out of the "leggings situation" and came to another, basically similar, district, where I found a basically similar building and climbed up a basically identical staircase. Then I pressed on the doorbell. Someone inside asked, "Who is it?"

"Delivery!" I replied. The door swung open at once, without the person behind even thinking to look through the peep-hole before opening up. I couldn't be sure if their sense of caution was rather poor or, on the other hand, whether they were overly anxious and laid great importance on the goods I was delivering.

Some time recently there was a story in the news about a woman who lived by herself and was killed by a courier. When the story came out, my colleagues, boss and I fell into some despondency, feeling generally uneasy. We believed that our trade would soon come off the rails, or that the number of items we delivered was sure to be cut massively. Instead, that the number never declined, but continued to grow and grow, so that our boss again became energized, and the online shopping at the crack of dawn on 11th November, China's "single's shopping day," saw huge discounts on online shopping websites, resulting in billions of dollars of purchases. It turned out to be a fierce battle of seckilling – the stock was literally wiped out in seconds. That was really an awesome spectacle.

Sometimes I was really bored, and then I fantasized about meeting some recipient for my deliveries who was not like everybody else. But there were none. Really. None at all. This one standing before my eyes was the same old style – opening the parcel, lowering her eyes, and giving a quick scan, which counted as having checked the item. She then peeped out, "Hmph," and signed.

I didn't know what she meant by that "hmph," but at any rate I didn't care what it was that I was delivering. The strips from the receipt to any item that we delivered, both the strip left in my hand at the end and the strip stuck on the parcel to be left with the recipient, had a description of the contents written on them. Still, I didn't have the time or the desire to take a look at the things I was passing along every day. I cared only about the delivery, not the story behind it, and certainly not the expression of the recipient when taking the goods. It had nothing to do with me whether this woman felt a sense of disappointment regarding her parcel. She signed, so my job was done, and I could go. At least you could say I made a fairer break for it than the case of the leggings, when the recipient proved so unwilling to inspect.

I could not have imagined at this time that her ill feelings would rebound onto me three days after completing this delivery.

I received a phone call from a lady. "How come my delivery hasn't arrived yet " she asked.

Such events were by no means rare – they came around frequently – and I didn't feel anxious myself. First I asked her what the situation was. She explained that I gave her a call on the morning two days previously, saying I'd be right over, but I had not actually come around even after two days.

What was a character! She had waited two days before giving me a call. She was by no means in a rush. I thought back to my work two days earlier. Nothing had been left out. I had completed all of my responsibilities on that day. I still didn't feel anxious, so asked if she was certain I was the one who had called when she picked up the phone two days earlier.

"Of course," she said. "I've still got your number on my phone. If not, how could I have called you? Luckily I kept it, actually. Otherwise I wouldn't know who to turn to."

The point she made here was wrong, or at least not one-hundred-percent correct. If she didn't receive some delivery, the problem might not lie entirely with the courier. It was always possible that something had gone wrong at some other point along the chain. Still, I could understand, since these women didn't know the structure of the delivery companies, nor could they see how our outfit was run. She couldn't imagine what our warehouse or our distribution center was like. All she could see was the delivery guy, and if she wasn't to ask me, then who could she ask? At any rate, hadn't my phone number already fallen into her hands?

With great patience, I verified the problem with her once more, "You're saying I contacted you the day before yesterday and said that I'd be over right away with a courier delivery?"

"Yes," she said.

I was experienced in this job, so I checked up with her a second time. "Please state your address and the full name of the person taking the delivery."

As she gave her reply, I rushed to grab a pen, jotted the information down, and promised the speediest of responses. In such a situation, I should naturally work with the utmost speed. People like her, with what appeared to be an unhurried personality, were pretty fair to deal with. The hurried ones wouldn't even ask about the black and white, and they wouldn't discuss who was wrong and who was right before bringing their complaint to the company and drag the courier's life into a mess. Then, even if it became clear on some other day just whom the responsibility lay with, the courier had already lost his perfect image in the eyes of his boss. He already had a smear on him. Not really worth it, huh?

The receipts for deliveries from two days back had long been collected at the company, and, rushing against time, I returned there to check up on the papers. Hunting out the receipts, I went through them one by one. Absolutely nothing was left out. Every single piece of paper had been signed by someone. This proved that I myself was not in error. I made my return call to the lady, telling her that there was indeed a delivery made to her address, and that the goods had already been delivered, since the order had been signed for.

She responded with a sudden cry, "Aha," Then she went on, "It's been signed for? Impossible! There's no one here during the day apart from me."

"Well," I said, "it is written in black and white, so there's no denying the delivery."

"So odd! Who was it? Who signed for it?"

I took a look at the name, scribbled down like mad so that I had to strain my eyes to make it out. I told her so-and-so's name. She stalled for a moment before asking just who this so-and-so was.

"The person who signed at your home," I said. Afraid that she still couldn't understand, I clarified the situation once more, "That is to say, I delivered the goods to your home, and it's possible that you weren't in, but there was someone else who signed."

"It can't be," she said, adding that she didn't know this so-and-so. "She's not a member of our family. You delivered it to the wrong place."

Her tone throughout was quite calm and polite – but what was the use of being polite? After all, no matter how polite she was, I would still have to make the delivery. But where had that parcel got to? I felt as if my head were going to explode, but I cooled down quickly and forced the feeling to die down. Then I gave careful thought to where the possible error might lie. Considering that the wrong person signed for it, it would be obvious to check the address first. I was experienced at this after all, and yet, again, I checked the facts with the lady. That was it! A single-character had been mistaken in the address – Honghu Gardens had become Hongfu Gardens. With my rich experience I knew straightaway that this was a problem with the local dialect – people confused h's with f's in their pronunciation.

I was far more relaxed now. First, I thought, this was not my responsibility – that lay with the person who sent the parcel. The blame wouldn't be falling on me. Naturally, blame in this way couldn't fall on the intended recipient, either. So I made haste to conciliate her.

"Alright! No need for you to panic. I know where the problem is. I made the delivery to a wrong address provided by the person who sent your parcel. This is easy to sort out. I'll run over there and bring it back, then send it over to you."

"How thoughtless, making a mistake when they wrote the address!" she said. Of course I knew that she was not talking about me, so I calmed down again and hurried over to the mistaken address.

At that moment I was still quite unhurried. It was only too common for an address to be written wrong. Instances of wrongly spelt names also abounded, and there were a great number of other errors – some you wouldn't think of, but there wasn't any error that *someone* wouldn't make. There was this one, for instance, when I made a call to a recipient, asking, "Are you apartment so-and-so, Block Y, District Z, on such-and-such a number, on such-and-such a street?"

"That's me!" said the voice from the other end. "I'm right at home waiting for your delivery."

So I couriered along, and the person happily signed. Yet soon after, a call came demanding the very same goods. I said that it had already been delivered as requested and signed for, but the man hadn't received anything, far less signed anything, which truly was odd. After several rounds of wrangling, dragging on over a great period of time, which stirred us all up to the point of not knowing what on earth to do, we finally realized that the delivery had been made to the wrong city. Imagine there were two cities which somehow had districts with the same name, and not only that, but within those districts were identical street names and numberings on the doors. You'd think there was no way such a thing could happen, but it really did.

More often it was a case of a phone number of the intended recipient being written incorrectly. When you called that wrong number, amicable folk would tell you that you had dialed the wrong number, but dislikeable folk would tell you to "go fuck yourself." Could you return the compliment and tell them to "go fuck themselves" too? Of course not.

Whatever, the general situation was that it didn't matter if the sender and recipient were those actually intended or written wrongly, they were, each and every one, your God – it's just that these visible Gods were of a different kind from the true, invisible One.

Once I had a problem with my phone. It just wouldn't work. I knew the situation was urgent, so I rushed off to get it repaired. However, in the short space of time in between, just one hour, a client had already made a complaint to the company. My phone was off, the client said, and how could a courier have his phone off? This was "robber's logic." Could it not happen that we couriers might get involved in some unexpected situations – what if I fell victim to a car accident en route and passed out? Damn it! It'd probably be better not to get involved in a car accident. Anyway, regardless of any misfortune I encountered, they were God, and I was God's servant.

I reached that block in Hongfu Gardens. I ascended to the floor, knocked on the door of the room, and it opened to reveal an unfamiliar woman, looking at me somewhat confusedly. Even if I was supposed to have seen her but two days ago, I felt she was a stranger now. I couldn't recall the face of everybody I made a delivery to, so this was very normal. And, anyway, if I had such an exceptional memory, I probably wouldn't have to weather all this wind and rain doing such a job – I'd recommend myself as a spy to the intelligence services.

But it didn't matter whether or not this woman was a stranger to me, and I wouldn't come to ask for her in particular. I was here to ask her to return a parcel that had been delivered in error, and I made a clean breast of it with her. As I spoke, she shook her head. Having shaken her head right through to the end of my speech, she said, "You've got it wrong. I didn't receive any parcels delivered by you."

"I came over here two days ago and handed you a delivery," I said, "and you signed it yourself." Although I suspected she was a stranger, I still had to get the upper hand over her at first. There was no alternative. Things had to go this way.

"You made a delivery here, and I received it?" she asked, doubtfully. "Did you see me? How it come I didn't see you?"

It wouldn't be wise to say that I had seen her, but I dared not deny either. I switched into a different mode of questioning. "Well then," I asked, "do you do a lot of internet and TV shopping?"

"Yes," she said. "I receive courier deliveries often, but not from you."

Things were okay as long as she admitted that she had received the parcel, and so, at this point, I took out my receipt and handed it to her. "Take a look," I said. "Isn't this your address?"

She took a look, and said, in a slightly surprised tone, "Ai, it is my address. But it wasn't me who received the delivery."

Without waiting for me to ask any more questions, she then took a step forward and pointed out the crux of the problem. "It's just that I am not the one who received the delivery," she said. "I didn't sign for it either. Neither the name nor the writing is mine."

I had been totally confident that this little mistake would be solved by rushing back to the mistaken address and putting things straight. How could I have known that the situation would grow even more complicated? My head began to explode once again. Fortunately, she was quite understanding.

"Yes." She said, "Nowadays it's not easy being a courier. It's very easy to make mistakes, and we've all become so careless." It appeared that she was keenly aware of the fix I was in, and was thus formulating an idea. "If you don't believe me, you take out some paper and I'll sign the name for you to compare, so you can see whether or not the writing's mine."

Having no other plan of my own, I could only go along with this, though I knew it would make me come off as a deeply suspicious and mean person. But you couldn't be too sure. In this line of work, you had no choice but to be this way. Otherwise, you would pay for a split-second of carelessness with your own bankruptcy. Even for a cash-on-delivery order, you may not lose money if it went wrong, but it would invariably cost you something – time, effort, or your good name. At the end of the day, you had to pay in some way.

She wrote her name down on the paper, and I was certain, even after a quick glance, that the courier's receipt in my hand was not signed by her. Seeing that I was not saying anything and, believing that I couldn't make the distinction, she said, pointing earnestly at her signature, "See for yourself. This writing is totally different. And anyway, if I had signed it, why would I want to deny it? There's no point doing that."

Although I could tell with a mere glance that the writing on my receipt was not hers, I remained unsatisfied. One could not be so easily satisfied. As soon as you felt satisfied, there would be no room left to negotiate – there would be no way out. I changed tack once more, asking, "Could it be that you weren't at home and this was signed by someone in your family?"

"No one from my family would be around during the day," she said, "and anyway, there's nobody with that name here." She looked at my face, now wrapped in bewilderment, then asked, "What was it you were delivering? Something valuable?"

"It would appear not," I said. "It was not insured – just a mop bought off a television ad."

"Well then," she said, "there's no way someone would have posed to get hold of that. What's the point in doing so for a mop? Is it worth it?"

"But," I said, "but, where can the mop have got to?"

She had been quite nice all along. Yet I still had my doubts about her.

She finally started to show some displeasure at this point. She took me to task. "You've got a bit of a problem. The recipient on your paper was obviously Tom, and you went and gave it to Dick or Harry to sign and receive. You didn't even bother to put down on the receipt that one did this in another's stead."

I couldn't agree with her argument. My company didn't stipulate that the delivery had to be signed by the person it was addressed to – it was perfectly suitable for family members to receive an item in his or her stead. But whatever, if someone had set his mind on posing to take a delivery, demanding that to be written down was about as useful as a fart.

So odd, when I thought about it. Although the courier service saw many strange things, I myself was cautious by nature, and I knew that it was tough to hold onto my rice bowl, so generally, I just didn't make mistakes. Where on earth could the problem lie in this instance? I took a second to organize my thoughts. First of all, the sender wrote the district name wrong. Then, naturally, I made my delivery in accordance with the given address. This was Stage One, and I had made no mistakes here. In Stage Two, there were no mistakes with the phone-number. I got the connection and the recipient picked up the phone, then waited for me to come with my delivery. So, no mistakes with Stage Two. In Stage Three, I headed off to the wrong address as provided by our sender, where there was, in fact, somebody waiting for a courier, and that guy signed for it. Although the name he gave was not that of the actual recipient, they still lived under the same roof, so there couldn't be any mistakes here. This was Stage Three, and I was still blameless.

If I had made no mistakes, then there would not have been an error in the delivery. So where could the mop have got to?

Again I tried to stir up some previous experience or training, and I had another hard think. Perhaps I had gone to the wrong floor? Maybe I had meant to go to the fifth, but with an unconscious slip into laziness, had left out a floor and ended up on the fourth? Or I could have gone into the wrong building, taken block number three for block number two – that was possible, as well. Or perhaps I had not actually come to the right district, but some other one?

Everything was very similar from district to district, from block to block, and from floor to floor.

When this thought came to me, I was immediately scared out of my wits. It was just like what I had seen in my dreams, one district after another, all the same. But I followed the instructions to the letter, so could it really happen that I had taken one address and wandered over to another one? And if I had never been to that district, how could it be that I had this memory of it? Could it be that I'd gone there in my dream?

Could it be that those events in my dream were truer than what had gone on in reality?

I wouldn't dare to say that it was impossible. Anything was possible.

It was just that, as things stood now, there was not a single piece of evidence to prove which mistake I had made.

I thought back to the scene, two days earlier, when I made the delivery. It occurred to me in a flash. I had an encounter with a familiar face in that district, and we even had a conversation on the road. All I had to do was to find that person and the pieces would fall into place.

In reality, I was a long way from any of the pieces slotting in.

I was always a patient person, so it was rare for me to make mistakes. But anybody who makes mistakes rarely will act more impatiently than one frequently in error when he does make a mess of things. I was this type of person. I was slightly impatient now, not because of some lost mop, but rather on account of my sense of responsibility for the job, and on account of my memory. Between the two, the latter was more important – if I could not remember some event from two or three days back, how could I help but break out in a cold sweat from head to toe?

I was impatient. Once I got impatient, the name behind that familiar face I encountered was completely forgotten. I made a great effort to recall the name, striving to fish out the concrete identity of this man from my jumbled brain. Who the hell was he? A family member? A classmate? A friend? A colleague? A relative? A neighbor? I supposed it was alright, since a loser like me wouldn't have too many people that he was close to. I searched through the directory on my phone, matching names with the appearance of the person in my memory, hoping that this would enlighten me. At first, every name that passed my eyes seemed to resemble the person, but, looking again, I thought that none of them really fit at all.

With no fear for the trouble it would bring, I started asking around, inquiring of everyone, one after another, who might turn out to be that person. Some just couldn't understand and ignored me, and some who seemed to understand thought it was all quite odd.

"What district? Never heard of it."

"What would I be doing going there? Do you think I'm having some bit on the side?"

"What are you driving at?" some others asked. "It's not April Fool's Day. And even if it were, couldn't you make the joke a little funnier?"

One went even further. "Are you stalking me? Who put you up to this? I know who has made you do this even if you don't tell me. It must so-and-so."

Hearing this, I was afraid that these efforts might end up with someone getting killed – best put a stop to it.

As things developed in this vein, I became even more impatient. Any further, and it would go pretty pear-shaped. By now I had even forgotten the appearance of the person who had talked to me in the district. And I was even more at a loose end as to what we had actually talked about. I was burning with impatience. I was afraid that this person, though undoubtedly not a ghost, would disappear into thin air, as if he had never existed.

Seeing that I was clutching at straws, a colleague gave a timely reminder. "Go and have a look at the housing estate's security video. As long as you were standing in the right place, they might have recorded you and that person."

This advice made me happier than any I could have hoped for, and I scampered off to the estate management office. But the management said the security video recording was not just for anyone to watch. You had to have the police come, or at the very least you had to have some documentation provided by the police.

But setbacks would not get the better of me at this stage. May as well go and find someone to help. I contacted the police, who asked me what business I did that I had to look at the recording.

"Well," I said, "I'm a courier and I lost my mop."

The police thought I was joking with them, and I got a real scolding. I was not afraid of getting an earful, not even a few swings. So I pled with them once more, explaining what had happened in precise detail. Losing a mop might be a small matter, but losing your rice bowl was a big problem. And finally, I won the expected sympathy.

"You couriers haven't got it easy by any means," said one of the police-officers who seemed to particularly understand me. "Nowadays, there really are too many deliveries made. My wife's become addicted to it. She buys things every day. Sometimes she won't even open the parcel, or she'll open one and then throw it away and go and buy it again. It kills me!"

Boosted by this piece of sympathy from the police, I could now, finally, take a look at the housing estate's video recording. Management, too, had become awfully friendly, helping me fast-forward here, rewind there, tracking down the moment of my arrival as I dictated it to them, then looking through once more, slowly... my God! There I was!

So I really did come to this district. I was alarmed by myself, noticing the great number of parcels strapped around my electric moped. If it were not me, but someone else, in that video, I would be sure to feel worried for him. How could such a feather-light vehicle carry so much cargo?

But that was exactly what I had been doing, only that I could not see what was piled up right there behind me when I was riding along on my electric moped.

I kept watching. Onwards I followed my movements. Lord Almighty! I was actually looking at the person I met here. It was my grandfather.

I was not supposed to be afraid. My grandfather had been dead for three years. I had bumped into my grandfather who departed from this world all that time ago. But if I was not afraid, there would be even less reason for you to be.

Everyone says that anything can happen in today's world, so what's there to say that there wouldn't be instances of resurrection?

My grandfather was wearing his green postman's uniform, pushing his bicycle, on top of which were strapped paper parcels big and small. However, there was nothing strange about all this – my grandfather was a postman in his younger days. In fact, when I started off as a courier, my mother cursed me, saying, "A dragon's child is a dragon, a phoenix's child is a phoenix, and the sons of mice nibble holes in walls."

I decided to hit a cruel nail on the head and so I returned the abuse with a wry joke. "So I am grandpa's boy then?"

This made my mother chuckle despite her anger. Now, although my grandfather's appearance at this point hadn't struck me as odd, there were still a few questions that I couldn't answer. On the security camera footage, I spoke to my grandfather.

"You're so old. Why haven't you retired?" I asked.

"I had retired," he said, "but then they said that there weren't enough hands on deck, so those of us who'd since been allowed to take a break all came out to lend a hand."

I thought about this, and it seemed perfectly reasonable. So those couriers bustling around the streets and byways, laden with parcels for delivery, weren't the whole story – there was a portion that you had not seen. This was what I was thinking, when my grandfather started to speak to me again.

"Life in these modern days is really convenient. Even if you buy something from the US, you'll receive it within a few days. It's nothing like in the past, when you had to wait over ten days, perhaps even half a month, just for ordinary surface mail!"

"That's right," I said. "Even the word 'speed' doesn't do it justice."

"It's called 'shuttling through time,'" said Grandfather.

I was just thinking that I should congratulate him on this fashionable expression, when he started talking again. "It's almost the Lunar New Year. I want to buy a present and have it delivered to your grandmother."

This really stunned me. "My grandmother?" I asked. "But hasn't she been gone for over twenty years? Could she receive your gift?"

"Nowadays all of us are leading a good life! Tell me, in these days, is there anything that we can't do?"

Having uttered these few words, Grandfather started to push his bike and make his deliveries. I could see why he did this – being advanced in years, he could not ride his bike when it was stacked with so many goods. He could only push it along as he went.

I went home and told my mother how I saw Grandfather three days ago in so-and-so district. She threw a "Bah!" in my direction before deriding me. "What the hell are you dreaming about?"

It was this "Bah!" that threw me into a state of confusion – or perhaps should I say that it brought me, with a start, back to consciousness? Perhaps everything that happened in that district was a dream of my creation. I could never be sure I was awake until my phone started to ring. Yet, I still remained somewhat doubtful about it – people could make and receive phone calls in their dreams, and I happened to have frequent dreams in which I was calling someone. These were as vivid as anything in real life – pressing buttons on the keypad, picking up and listening to the other end, and my own speaking – all indistinguishable from what I would do in my conscious state.

This call is from the lady who should have received her mop. She had received it, she said, but still wished to thank me. I was astonished. It taxed the brain to think that she had already taken delivery of it when I hadn't even gone looking for the mop, and what mop of all mops was this mop anyway? Was it that some good-hearted soul sensed the mess I was in and so offered a new one, or was it that some other careless sender who had written his address wrong, an error which happened to bring it to the lady's address, with the result that someone else's mop had been sent to her home? Or was it that my grandfather who, hating to see all this trouble I'd been going through, had concealed himself somewhere and played a magician's trick?

Who knows what it was all about? At the end of the day, the mop had arrived, and it had nothing to do with me anymore. Quickly, I pushed the mop to the back of my mind. As long as there was no more chasing me down as if it was my responsibility, then everything was okay.

I returned to the company and took on another pile of consignments. Lowering my head to take a look at the strips of paper, I saw one address for delivery written on the first receipt, *Reverie Gardens*.

So I set off toward Reverie Gardens.

THE CREATIVITY, PEACE, AND FREEDOM IN THE PROCESS OF WRITING

<small>AN INTERVIEW WITH FAN XIAOQING</small>

By **Yang Haocheng**
Translated by **Helen Wang**

YANG HAOCHENG: We know that you graduated from the Chinese Department of Soochow University, and that you stayed on as a teacher for a while after graduation. It's said that all university students in Chinese departments want to be writers. Was this true in your case? Then you became a professional writer – was it because given the choice between being a teacher and a writer, you preferred creative writing? If you were to live your life again, would you still choose to be a writer? Or would you choose something else?

FAN XIAOQING: Many university students in Chinese departments dream of being a writer, and many of them try their hand at writing. This was certainly true for students of my own and earlier generations. Whether it's true for students of Chinese Literature now, I don't really know. In my case, the dream of being a writer started when I was at university. Before going to university, I hadn't read many books, in fact hardly any at all, because there weren't any books available for me to read. But when I went to university, I read a huge amount, especially in the first and second years, when I read pretty much all the classics of world literature in the library. It was so inspiring. At the same time, in the late' 70s and' 80s, there was a nationwide craze for literature in literary circles, and that may have been the spark that lit my dream. I started writing novels in my second year, and in my third year, I published my debut novel.

As for choosing between teacher and writer, I prefer writing. I had no hesitation in leaving the university and starting a career as a writer.

Since the beginning of the' 80s, my life has been about writing. I haven't really tried any other occupations, so it's hard to compare. If I were to do some other work instead of writing, it might be a better fit than writing, or it might be a disaster. It's hard to know. So, I can't really answer your question about choice. From that perspective, I suppose my life might appear a bit monotonous.

YANG HAOCHENG: You are a hardworking, prolific writer. You write about different subject matters, and in different genres and styles. Are there any works which you consider to be representative? Thinking about your rich creative output – and leaving aside comments from readers and critics – are you satisfied? Have your works achieved what you wanted them to achieve? And if not, why not?

FAN XIAOQING: I have written a lot, and there are some pieces that are quite special to me, but it's strange how the things I like keep changing. In terms of representative works, we could talk about different styles. If we look simply at my short stories, we could say "Rui Yun" in the 1980s, "Ying Yang Alley" in the late

1990s, and more recently "City Living, Country Living" are all representative works, but each one is quite unique.

On the whole, I'm satisfied with what I've written. Maybe it's because I've written so much that I can always find something that I think I've written well and am happy with. There are some pieces that achieved what I wanted to achieve. But ideals and ambitions change, and the ideals and ambitions of yesterday aren't always the same today. Writing is a process of constantly chasing change and creating new things. Looking at things in this way, my works might seem a long way from my ideal, because my ideal is always developing.

YANG HAOCHENG: Your works – your novels, novellas, and short stories – don't have big, sweeping narratives. They are mostly quite modest, delicate, sometimes clever, even garrulous, stories that develop with the flow of language. Do you think this comes from your personality or from the fact that you are a woman?

FAN XIAOQING: When I first started writing, I didn't pay too much attention to style, so it probably comes from there. In my first pieces, I wrote as I pleased about whatever I liked. The subject matter of my earliest writings was mostly about old Suzhou, with that kind of quiet, peaceful background, and often the content influenced the form, and the writing had a kind of easy feel to it, like going for a gentle stroll. At the same time, I suppose this style must also be linked to my personality and to my being a woman.

YANG HAOCHENG: I'm quite intrigued by your style of writing. The language offers no surprises, there's no suspense, and the plot has no particular highs and lows. You don't make people laugh or cry. It's more the plain narrative style of everyday conversation.

These factors make it very difficult to please readers and critics, especially given the limitless variety of information, knowledge, and entertainment that is available in today's society. How do you view this issue? Of course, we can say that a writer doesn't write to win prizes or to please other people, but if you yourself are aware of this and of the need to "move with the times," would you choose to hold your ground or to "move with the times?" Of course, I'm not suggesting that you should – the choice is entirely yours.

FAN XIAOQING: This issue has been troubling me for a long time now, and it's one I've been exploring and looking for an answer to. But practical experience tells me that there won't be a clear-cut answer. I'm more inclined to believe that writers have to listen to their inner voice. At the same time, as a writer, you have a desire for change that is with you all your life. You talk about there being a choice between holding one's ground and "moving with the times," but "moving with the times" is not necessarily progress. In fact, whenever I've made changes in my novels, there have been people who hailed them, but there also have been people who complained, or sighed with regret, or even criticized them. And at those times, I swing back and forth with self-doubt, but when I pick up my pen and start writing again, I have to listen to my own inner voice. It's a case of changing while you hold your ground, and holding your ground while you change.

YANG HAOCHENG: While we're on this subject, do you pay much attention to what the outside world thinks of your work? Or, to put it another way, does what the outside world thinks have an influence over your creative writing?

Fan Xiaoqing: Of course I pay attention to this, and I very much hope that people pay attention to my work. I consider the responses of the outside world very carefully, but I don't heed them or reject them blindly. Whatever enters my heart becomes part of my inner voice, and I will listen accordingly. But if something doesn't enter my heart, it will probably just blow over me.

Yang Haocheng: As a number of commentaries have pointed out, many of your works, especially the short pieces, can be seen as sharing a "searching" theme. I'm thinking of "The Hallucinated Courier" (published in the first issue of *Chinese Arts and Letters*) and the pieces you sent me subsequently, such as "Where Did I Lose You?", "Who Did I Meet in the Neighborhood?", "Tenant," "Tea Trees at Yougang," and "Born in an Unknown Hour." Your two pieces in this issue of *Chinese Arts and Letters* – "City Living, Country Living" and "Ying Yang Alley" – are both concerned with a search. What is it that draws you to this theme? Also, in many of your works, the status of the characters is very vague. We may not know their names, or whether they are male or female, or whether a brother is older or younger, or whether they are "born at dusk or dawn." These things appear not to be important. Such characterization is quite different from traditional writing methods. Have you done this intentionally? Can it be seen as an attempt at postmodernism? Are you trying through this lack of status in the characterization to give readers some kind of cultural or philosophical message?

Fan Xiaoqing: Actually, the theme of searching and the imprecise characterization are closely linked. We are in the process of developing a material society, but the new order is not yet properly established, and the old order has not completely disappeared, so we're at a stage in between old and new, when there are lots of contradictory, or even absurd, things. It's a feature of contemporary society, and particularly of Chinese society. For example, recently everyone has experienced phenomena like being required to prove that your mother is your mother, or being forced to go on constant searches to prove some fact that is already very clear. There are many people and many things that are impossible to understand, and they raise doubts in my mind about this society. Do we still have a fairly stable standard of values and behaviour or not? Human society should move forward in accordance with certain rules, but the reality is often not like that. Our society is filled with so many uncertainties, and things that people feel cannot be trusted. We hear that the government cannot be trusted, businesses cannot be trusted, individuals cannot be trusted – how can it be that everyone feels this way? Every time I see a piece of news in the media, my first concern is not its content, but its authenticity. It's the same for most of the information posted on WeChat. There is so much doubt. The theme of searching is about looking for a standard of value. The imprecise characterization in my work is closely linked to this. My stories seldom describe the physical appearance of characters, because I feel these characters are only representatives, and that what they symbolize is greater than a character's reality. I'd say this is the dominant thinking behind the vagueness in many of my recent stories.

YANG HAOCHENG: I'm not sure how to place your stories. The accounts and descriptions seem to be real life things that we can actually feel or experience for ourselves, but at the same time, they seem to incorporate some non-rational, even "magical" components. This creates a feeling of being caught between reality and illusion, of not being sure whether you are on solid ground. I guess this is a common practice of artistic creation, but you certainly do not belong in the Writers of the Absurd, do you? It's all about the "degree" of rationality. Take Er Xiu from "Tea Trees at Yougang," for example. Simply by her teacher's poetic description of Yuluochun, gunpowder tea, the enchanted girl should be so obsessed with it that after her teacher dies in an accident, she feels compelled to go and find the grave where she believes her teacher is buried, then insists on staying in the teacher's hometown to be a tea-picker. I think readers may question the reality of your stories, even though truth in art doesn't need to completely match truth in reality. And the same is true, as some critics have pointed out, of Wang Cai, the protagonist in "City Living, Country Living," who feels compelled to move himself and his family to the city, simply to find out what essential oil is.

FAN XIAOQING: Yes, that was an issue. In fact, in "Tea Trees at Yougang," I also feel that the ending was a bit far-fetched. Just as you say, my stories are basically realist, so rationality is something that must be taken seriously. The rationality of both of these stories has been called into question, but the situations are quite different. Superficially, you can say that in "City Living, Country Living," Wang Cai went to the city for a bottle of "essential oil," but in fact that wasn't the full story, because there was a huge social background to this event, namely the phenomenon of migrant workers moving to the cities. Chinese society had developed to a point that the migrant worker phenomenon was inevitable. Wang Cai would still have gone to the city, even if he hadn't gone for the "essential oil." There isn't the same sense of inevitability in "Tea Trees at Yougang." If I were a magic realism or surrealist writer, then a lack of rationality would be acceptable, but I'm not. I need to take more care over such things in future.

YANG HAOCHENG: Would you tell us a little about the stories in this issue? – "City Living, Country Living," "Ying Yang Alley," and "Born in an Unknown Hour"? What inspired you to write stories like these?

FAN XIAOQING: We've already touched on "City Living, Country Living," and the background is, of course, the phenomenon of migrant workers. The influx of migrant workers to the city over a decade ago affected our lives, both directly and indirectly, and as the various effects began to accumulate, I found I had to go and focus on their lives. The basic framework of the story, including the section about the "essential oil," is fictional. As for inspiration, Ziqing is a shadow of myself, because like Ziqing, I have the habit of keeping a close eye on family expenses. Writing a story like that was a gradual, cumulative process of thinking and development. It was not the result of suddenly being inspired.

There's more of a story behind "Ying Yang Alley." I was researching the people and customs of my hometown, Suzhou, and by chance came across a story of Mrs Zhang Taiyan (章太炎) in a historical document. The account was very short. It said that she was once the campus queen of a girls' school in

Shanghai, and that she was clever as well as beautiful. Mrs Tang is based on her. No one else was mentioned in the document. I added the other old ladies and Mr Mai, who came looking for her. They are fictional characters. I am familiar with life in the little streets of Suzhou, and I wanted to show through the story that behind very ordinary things there have often been great waves. This old lady in her twilight years, tucked away in the little lanes of Suzhou, quietly chatting with a group of people of her age – who would imagine she once had such a dazzling youth? And yet she had.

YANG HAOCHENG: I myself like "Ying Yang Alley" very much. The story is very simple, and at the same time very beautiful. To think that someone can hold a dream from their youth, and cherish it their entire life until it comes true, is quite special.

FAN XIAOQING: Yes, it's rare that something like that happens. I can tell you about the inspiration behind "Born in an Unknown Hour" as well. I was in a car with some friends, and one of them said he could tell whether the official year of one's birth was accurate or not. It was completely unexpected, and I thought about my family, in which three out of five people share the same birthday, February 1. In fact, no one in the family was born on that day. When we were little, birthdays weren't important. Any date would do. It didn't matter if your birthday was accurate or not. It's not as important as it is today, when birthdays have a direct bearing on promotion and pension, and so on. My mother told me that I was born on July 22. She said I was born at dusk, because it was a summer evening, and she had just seen the lights coming on outside. But somehow my birth date on my ID card has always been February 1. I never bothered to change it, because there didn't seem to be any point in going to all the trouble of working it out exactly. I'm not the only one. There are many cases like mine. It made me think about the absurdity and uncertainty of life, and I wrote it up as a story.

YANG HAOCHENG: In this issue of *Chinese Arts and Letters*, we are publishing three of your short stories. In fact, one of them, "City Living, Country Living," you gave to us when we were setting up the journal. I wanted to publish it then and there, but I happened to see that an English translation had been published in an American magazine, *Chinese Literature Today*, and I needed some time to check if there were any copyright issues. This story reflects ordinary grassroots life, but through this small setting we see a much bigger picture, the evolution of city and country life in China today. It has the qualities of a classic, and there is wisdom and humor in the clever ending, which makes the reader smile with recognition. The second one, "Ying Yang Alley," is characterized by its calmness. Nothing jars. There is a long, soothing timelessness, and from the calmness emerges the beauty of life. It's rather like a beautiful essay or a poem. But, if I may be so bold, it seems that most writing of this kind is fleeting – there are not many such memorable pieces. For a long time, people have emphasized the classical nature of literary works, and it's my personal belief that such emphasis does not date, and will not date in the future. Certain works, ancient and modern, have become classics because of their vivid and idiosyncratic characters – Lin Daiyu (林黛玉) and Jia Baoyu (贾宝玉), Ah Q (阿Q) and Kong Yiji (孔乙己), Hamlet and Macbeth, Huckleberry Finn, and Santiago in *The Old Man and the Sea* are all strong characters. These days, after modernism and postmodernism, many writers (and artists) have chosen to focus on form – and so we have, for example, James Joyce's stream of consciousness and Gertrude Stein's obsession with repetition and sound. These works stand out. They catch our attention. We can say that they are unique in the long tradition of literature, and we can also say that they create a kind of new tradition. So it seems that great characterization and a unique writing style are the most common routes to establishing a writer's individual status, and if a writer can take these qualities to the ultimate stage, then he has a classic. Would you agree with this? In your many works, how would you evaluate your characterization and writing methods? I think that, whether they acknowledge it or not, every writer, deep down, must dream of their work standing out as a classic one day. Do you have such a dream? Do you think that any of your works might become classics?

FAN XIAOQING: That's a very interesting question, and a very stimulating one. On the question of classics, we can ask about characterization in modern novel writing and the continuation of that tradition. Modern and contemporary fiction isn't always about a particular person. Sometimes it is only through someone whose identity really doesn't matter that the absurdity and uncertainty of modern and contemporary society are conveyed. For example, in my own writing of the last few years, none of the characters in my stories are important per se, and sometimes I don't care if they are male or female, or what they look like. The important thing is how their personal history and experiences represent the commonality of contemporary society. This is a far cry from traditional classical literature and characterization. I often wonder whether I should return to a stronger characterization. It's an important question, but, for the time being, I don't seem to be able to answer it.

As for one's work standing out as a classic, I'm sure that's what every writer desires. But, as with winning prizes, such an achievement is not solely dependent on an individual's ability. For me, it is more the creativity, peace, and freedom in the process of writing that I enjoy.

YANG HAOCHENG: In your works, there is a very clear sense of place, and Suzhou, your hometown, is rather like a birthmark on many of your works, particularly your early works. This is true for many writers, including Thomas Hardy, Mark Twain, and William Faulkner, and our own Mo Yan (莫言), Jia Pingwa (贾平凹), and Wang Shuo (王朔). Do you think you have written all there is to say about Suzhou? You made your name writing about people and matters in Suzhou, and now, when you look back, do you think that the strong sense of place made you a success, or limited you?

FAN XIAOQING: As you say, Suzhou is like a visible birthmark on my early works. I wrote about the people of Suzhou, about Suzhou as a place, about things that happened in Suzhou, and I wrote using the local language of Suzhou. That kind of writing, at that time, did bring me success. At least, everyone knew I was writing about Suzhou. In my later works, I gradually tried to make the birthmark less visible, perhaps because I didn't want to be so tightly bound by place and wanted to loosen the hold a bit. But, even if the birthmark is less apparent, the spirit is still that of Suzhou, at least that of southern Jiangsu. For example, if I write about a migrant worker, he'll be working in Suzhou rather than in a northern city. Once the local water and earth has nourished your writing style, it's very difficult to change it completely. Suzhou is my hometown. Have I written all there is to say about it? Actually, I'm a long way from that, so maybe, in a few more years, I might go back to writing about it.

Yang Haocheng: I'm not a writer, but I dare say that writing is like any other profession, in that it's not easy to excel. What is the hardest aspect of writing for you? Or, maybe I should say, when you are writing, what troubles you the most?

Fan Xiaoqing: It's still a question of creating new things. Writers can't always be repeating themselves, or they and their readers will get bored. I've produced rather a lot, which is both a good and a bad thing. But I have come to realize now that a huge output might be more of a problem than a blessing. If you write a lot at a particular time, it's likely that those pieces may be very similar. For example, I've recently been interested in absurdity and uncertainty, but if I write a lot all in one go, a single piece might seem quite good, but a lot of similar pieces will cause people to complain that they're all the same. So, for writers like me with a high output, the key questions are how to draw a distance between works, and how not to repeat oneself. These are both frustrations I have when I am writing, and problems that I must resolve. Fortunately, I've now started to slow down a bit and grind away slowly at each piece, doing my best to keep people from getting tired of them.

Yang Haocheng: You've spoken previously of your love for the beauty of moderation and how this guides your writing. There are no great ups and downs in your stories, nor great joy or great despair. But in society there is light and dark, and in life there is suffering and joy. Moderation as a life attitude may be a lofty spiritual realm for one to attain, but in artistic creation, it might give people a feeling of mediocrity, neither high nor low, neither hot nor cold, neither good nor bad. Have you ever considered that exposing darkness and suffering as compared to the narrative of joy and light might lend more tension to your writing?

FAN XIAOQING: I agree with your point of view. Art needs to have impact, and it needs strength, or it's difficult to move readers. But my writing is rather restrained. I'm hoping for a light touch. It's my personal preference, if you like. Often, at critical moments, I can't resist putting pen to paper, but then I'll suddenly pull myself back and stop. There are always some people who feel my writing lacks passion, but I like it this way and believe that it is no less valid a state of being. I write like this intentionally. Many critics have also said that my works leave them feeling unsatisfied at the end. Of course, whether I can provide them with a satisfactory end or not, the first question is whether I have that writing ability, and the second is whether I am willing to change the way I write. If I change and do not like the result, then I think it's better not to change.

YANG HAOCHENG: This issue of *Chinese Arts and Letters* has a critical essay by Wang Yao on your "transition." This is more or less a definition of your writing by critics. Do you agree with what he says? Have you made a conscious transition? And if so, what prompted you to make it? And how do you rate the results of the transition?

Fan Xiaoqing: I have to acknowledge that there has been a transition. Of course, it has taken place subconsciously. It was not a case of deciding that one day there would be a transition, and so it happened. Sometimes, when I am writing away, I look back, and discover that there is something different from before. My life now is very different from before. The heavy but tedious administrative work determines that I cannot write as leisurely as I used to. I can no longer write pieces like "Ying Yang Alley." Often I will be at a meeting all morning, and in the afternoon I will snatch whatever time I can to write, and because of this, the speed and rhythm of my writing have become faster. I think the transition must be linked with my life, and also, of course, with age. As for the results of the transition, it's not easy for me to judge. I can only say that before, as a professional writer, my life was quite calm and leisurely, my writing was unhurried, and I was relatively more at ease and at home writing on subject matters related to Suzhou. Today, because of work commitments, my writing is faster, and the pieces I write are tighter. Personally, I still prefer pieces like "Ying Yang Alley," but as for judging my works before and after transition, perhaps we should let the reader decide.

Yang Haocheng: In writing, we talk about the passion to write coming first, then about the actual writing. Some people believe that writing comes from personal experience and wide reading, while others believe that one must have a gift or talent to be a writer. Qian Zhongshu's (钱锺书) writing, both his academic and creative work, drew in large part upon his phenomenal breadth of reading. Shakespeare didn't read much, and yet he earned himself a place in history as a great writer. Which camp do you belong to? What connections between reading and writing do you see? Would you tell us a little about your own reading?

FAN XIAOQING: I don't read a huge amount, and my writing draws mostly on how I perceive life, on my sharp observation of life and on capturing the literary qualities of life. But I believe that reading provides the most power for writing. I would say there have been two stages of reading in my life. When I was younger, I focused on literary works. But later I turned to reading a greater variety of books, sometimes simply as reference for my own creative writing. My reading habit is not to force myself to read. For example, if I hear someone discussing a good book but can't get hold of a copy easily, then I won't go to a huge amount of trouble to get one. I think there's an element of fate in people and books coming together. If fate brings the book into my hands, then I'll read it.

YANG HAOCHENG: You're a professional writer, and you're also the Chair of Jiangsu Writers Association. As a writer, on the outside, you have to face the world, and inside, you have to face your own soul. To put it another way, a writer looks for truth. We all know that being a pure writer and the head of a writers association involves many awkward contradictions that are difficult to reconcile. Our Writers Association is an official organization, quite different from the club-like nature of writers' associations overseas. You are required to be both writer and official – two very different beasts. How do you find a happy balance between the two? Or, do you live a kind of double life? Perhaps, when you are writing, you feel an invisible force controlling you? If you had to choose, would you prefer to be loyal to your writing, or loyal to the institution's regulations?

FAN XIAOQING: Professor Yang, how can one answer that question?

YANG HAOCHENG: We could say that your life is basically in academia and officialdom, but what's interesting is that your choice of subject leans more towards ordinary people. It's usually the case that it's much easier for authors to manage characters who have lives familiar to their own, but you do the opposite. Is it a conscious decision? Or perhaps you are trying to avoid something?

FAN XIAOQING: I was born in Suzhou, then I moved with my parents to the countryside when I was twelve and just starting junior high school. It's a very sensitive age, when you sort of do and don't understand things. I was full of curiosity. I was plunged into the countryside. I went to the local school, and when I finished school in the county seat at eighteen, I was sent down to the countryside again. Six years of school with country children, and of close contact with country people, left a deep impression on me. I knew them, and later on, I wanted to write about them. Then I went to university and stayed on as a teacher and professional writer, and I began a different kind of life. But on the whole, there have been very few ups and downs in my life, and for a professional writer, this constitutes something of a limitation. In order to enrich my experience, and to have enough source material for writing, I consciously went back to the people of my hometown and worked for the local residents' committee and the local government, and I started to do some creative writing that reflected the lives of ordinary citizens.

You mentioned reflecting academia and officialdom in fiction. I've barely touched on academia in my writing and have written only a few pieces that concern officialdom, but there are some, including "Women Comrades" and two other long pieces in which I wrote about a few female cadres in officialdom, cadres in a small town, and cadres in the city. Why don't I write about academics? I think the reason may be because the people and their concerns are too close to my own. Life is richer than art. As a writer, I understand them too well. Understanding academics is like understanding myself, so if I write about them it's very likely that I would write too realistically, and you have to be careful or you'll have people trying to find their own places in your fiction. You can try transforming them by inventing extra things, but it wouldn't be as rich or as vivid as those people and their concerns are in real life. For example, if I write about a particular cultural organization, people will immediately know where I'm coming from, and they'll try to find their own places.

YANG HAOCHENG: Are you saying that it would be dangerous to write about those people? Are you afraid of getting into trouble?

FAN XIAOQING: Not really. I'm just scared that the reality of life might overwhelm the artistic creation. Life is the source of art, but there is a distance between art and life, and it's essential that there is this distance. For example, my stories about the countryside were not written immediately after I left there, but twenty or thirty years later, when there had been time for that material to settle and filter through. By then, I understood how to write about the life I had lived in the countryside. As for academia, I think it will be much the same, and if one day I have the ability to write about academics, then I will.

Yang Haocheng: The day before yesterday, a PhD student from the English Department at Harvard came to visit me at home. Her supervisor is one of the advisors to *Chinese Arts and Letters* and had recommended that her student contact me. We talked about Chinese culture and Chinese literature going out into the world, so the world can know about it, and how difficult that process of going out is. "The road will be long. Our climb will be steep." Neither officialdom nor individual writers can afford to take it for granted. Of course, there is hope, and we have three main considerations in mind concerning how we might achieve our ambition. First, the authors being promoted must have staying power, like Lu Xun (鲁迅), whose appeal hasn't diminished over the last half century. Second, we must promote them in foreign language media, which must be of good quality and must succeed in conveying the essence of the original. Third, we must consolidate our efforts. A single translation is not enough, nor is the translation of one single aspect. We need to take our strongest works and repeatedly promote them in a range of media, making an impact in this way, a very deep impression. In your roles as writer and Chair of Jiangsu Writers Association, how do you see Chinese literature going out into the world? What kind of impact did Mo Yan's winning of the Nobel Prize have on you and any other writers that you know?

Fan Xiaoqing: I completely agree with you on these three points, especially on the second and third ones. It is absolutely right that foreign language editions "must succeed in conveying the essence of the original" and that we must strive to deliver them repeatedly and in different media, so that the impact will be felt. This is what you are doing now, and in this respect, on behalf of Jiangsu Writers Association and Jiangsu writers generally, I'd like to express our greatest respect and sincere gratitude to you and your team. Mo Yan's winning the Nobel Prize certainly validates this point of view. For powerful yet modest introverts, as the majority of Chinese writers are, this is so necessary and truly inspirational.

About Yang Haocheng

Born in Yixing, Jiangsu Province, in October 1963, Yang Haocheng held a PhD and was a professor, a translator, a calligrapher, and the editor in chief of the all-English magazine *Chinese Arts and Letters*. He worked at the School of Foreign Languages and Cultures of Nanjing Normal University, mainly teaching Translation of Literary Classics, Western Civilization, and A Survey of Chinese Culture. His field of research and research interests included American culture and literature, modern Chinese literature, literature translation, western art theory and history, and Chinese calligraphy. His publications include *Mao Iconology, The East Is Dawning-Personality Pursuit in the New Culture Movement, Highlights of Chinese Calligraphy, Gulliver's Travels, Lolita, The Silence of the Lambs, Cat's Eye, Giants: The Parallel Lives of Frederick Douglas and Abraham Lincoln, The Old Man and the Sea, The Story of Modern Art,* and *Odes to Jiangsu by Renowned Poets through the Ages* (English translation of classical Chinese poems). Cf

ABOUT THE AUTHOR

FAN XIAOQING, A native of Suzhou, Jiangsu Province, Fan Xiaoqing was born into a family of intellectuals in Songjiang, Shanghai, in 1955. After graduating from the Chinese Department of Soochow University in 1982, she became a teacher of literary theory at her alma mater, but soon found herself more interested in writing than teaching, and so switched to professional writing three years later. Fan is a diligent, prolific writer. She has published over sixteen novels, seven collections of prose, and numerous short stories. Her *Romance from Kudang Alley, A Hundred Days of Sunshine, Urban Expressions, Women Comrades,* "City Living, Country Living," "Rui Yun," "Ying Yang Alley," and other works have not only won great critical acclaim, but are also widely popular with readers young and old. Fan Xiaoqing is now on her third term in office as the Chair of Jiangsu Writers Association.